Young Children Visit Museums

Bringing different cultural perspectives on creativity with them, teachers and children in two early childhood education sites in Aotearoa New Zealand were using museum visits as jumping-off places to hone their creative capacity building.

As a contribution to Tim Ingold's discussion of anthropology and/ as education, and also finding John Dewey's writing valuable (specifically his framing of "enduring attitudes"), the authors employ a navigation metaphor throughout the discussion. They describe a coming together of four Cultural Anchors (thinking from materials) with four Coordinates (creative capacity builders) to describe ways in which the children were making creative sense of the museum exhibits, while at the same time gathering information about them. They take these travel metaphors from a star cluster in the southern hemisphere night sky, Matariki, which provided early sea-going Māori with guidance as they navigated wide stretches of ocean in their sea-going canoes to reach Aotearoa New Zealand.

A Māori immersion early childhood centre and school, and a New Zealand kindergarten provided lively examples of children's and teachers' responses to the treasured artefacts (taonga) in their local museums. The book describes an ecosocial framing, from "little to big", and illustrates the different cultural perspectives on creativity. The Mana Tamariki kaiako (teachers) gifted us a title—He taonga, he rerenga arorangi (Where there are treasured objects, the spirit is nurtured and creativity will be inspired).

Margaret Carr is an Emeritus Professor in the Wilf Malcolm Institute of Educational Research at the University of Waikato in Aotearoa New Zealand, formerly a geographer at Victoria University of Wellington, a potter and an early childhood teacher. Margaret was a co-director of the project that developed the national early childhood curriculum, Te Whāriki, and has researched and written on early childhood, and learning stories as a narrative method of assessment.

Brenda Soutar, Tribal groups—Ngāti Porou and Ngāti Awa. Brenda is part of the group who established Mana Tamariki kōhanga and kura (Māori immersion early childhood centre and school), where she was a leader for several decades. She was also a member of the 2015 Ministerial-appointed Advisory Group on Early Learning. In 2016/2017, Brenda became a member of the writing group for the update of Te Whāriki, the national early childhood curriculum.

Leanne Clayton, Tribal groups—Te Āti Awa and Ngāti Rārua. Leanne is a leader at Mana Tamariki kōhanga reo in Palmerston North, Aotearoa New Zealand where she also teaches in the kōhanga reo (0–5 years) and previously in the kura (5–8 years). She also teaches in a Māori immersion early childhood degree programme at a tribal university, Te Wānanga o Raukawa, situated in Otaki, a nearby town.

Jeanette Clarkin-Phillips is a Senior Lecturer in Education at the University of Waikato. In several research projects on young children, she has explored the ways in which children form relationships with artefacts to make sense of the world and develop a deeper understanding of their citizenship. Her PhD case study thesis was a mapping of a kindergarten community as an affordance ecosystem. She has been actively involved in national early childhood teacher forums.

Bronwen Cowie is a Professor and an Associate Dean of Research at Te Kura Toi Tangata, the Division of Education at the University of Waikato. Her research has included formative assessment interactions in school classrooms; she has a particular interest in student voice and cultural responsiveness, curriculum implementation in science classrooms and collaborations with teachers and students. Bronwen has led a number of national projects using surveys complemented by case studies to highlight the situated nature of learning activities.

Shelley Butler, Tribal group—Ngati Kahu ki Whangaroa. Shelley is an early childhood teacher with experience in home- and centre-based early childhood contexts. During this museum project, Shelley was a teaching fellow at the University of Waikato and a research assistant at the Wilf Malcolm Institute of Educational Research. Shelley's passion for research in early childhood was enriched during this project in the collection, management and methods of analysis of the data.

Rethinking Education
Series Editors: Bernd Herzogenrath and Tim Ingold

In the face of the still dominant model of progressive education, the volumes in this series explore ways of thinking education otherwise – ways that give hope for coming generations and for the renewal of life. They offer visions for the future, manifestos, experimental curricula, speculative syllabi, and case studies of alternative education at work. They are short and provocative, intended for academics, researchers, professionals and students alike.

Young Children Visit Museums
Cultural and Creative Perspectives
Margaret Carr, Brenda Soutar, Jeanette Clarkin-Phillips, Leanne Clayton, Bronwen Cowie, and Shelley Butler

Cultures of Erudition and Desire in University Pedagogy
Thoughts on Practice-led Curricula Before, Through, and Beyond Deleuze
Lianna Psarologaki

For more information about this series, please visit https://www.routledge.com/Rethinking-Education/book-series/RETHED

Young Children Visit Museums
Cultural and Creative Perspectives

Margaret Carr, Brenda Soutar,
Leanne Clayton,
Jeanette Clarkin-Phillips,
Bronwen Cowie, and
Shelley Butler

LONDON AND NEW YORK

First published 2023
by Routledge
4 Park Square, Milton Park, Abingdon, Oxon OX14 4RN

and by Routledge
605 Third Avenue, New York, NY 10158

Routledge is an imprint of the Taylor & Francis Group, an informa business

© 2023 Margaret Carr, Brenda Soutar, Leanne Clayton, Jeanette Clarkin-Phillips, Bronwen Cowie, Shelley Butler

The right of Margaret Carr, Brenda Soutar, Leanne Clayton, Jeanette Clarkin-Phillips, Bronwen Cowie, Shelley Butler to be identified as authors of this work has been asserted in accordance with sections 77 and 78 of the Copyright, Designs and Patents Act 1988.

All rights reserved. No part of this book may be reprinted or reproduced or utilised in any form or by any electronic, mechanical, or other means, now known or hereafter invented, including photocopying and recording, or in any information storage or retrieval system, without permission in writing from the publishers.

Trademark notice: Product or corporate names may be trademarks or registered trademarks, and are used only for identification and explanation without intent to infringe.

British Library Cataloguing-in-Publication Data
A catalogue record for this book is available from the British Library

ISBN: 978-1-032-07842-7 (hbk)
ISBN: 978-1-032-32252-0 (pbk)
ISBN: 978-1-003-31360-1 (ebk)

DOI: 10.4324/9781003313601

Typeset in Times New Roman
by MPS Limited, Dehradun

Contents

List of Figures		viii
Rethinking Education: Series Editor Foreword		ix
Acknowledgements		xi
1	Culture, Context and Creativity	1
2	Thinking in Triangles	18
3	E Rangahau Ana: Gathering Information	33
4	E Whakawhanaunga Ana: Growing a Relationship	45
5	E Waihanga Ana: Imagining	56
6	E Whakaahua Ana: Using Multiple Modes	69
7	He Taonga, He Rerenga Arorangi	80
8	Creative Capacity Building: A Going On	89
	Index	108

Figures

2.1	Cultural Anchor 1	21
2.2	Cultural Anchor 2	22
2.3	Cultural Anchor 3	25
2.4	Cultural Anchor 4	27
3.1	Rangimatua: Drawing by Rakei Te Kura	40
4.1	Taumaihiroa's manu aute 1	48
4.2	Taumaihiroa's manu aute 2	48
4.3	Taumaihiroa's manu aute 3	48
4.4	Taumaihiroa's manu aute & Tāwhirimātea & Tamanuiterā	49
5.1	Sarah's drawing of the smiling dinosaur	63
5.2	Sarah's drawing of the witch's hat	65
7.1	Rangimatua: Drawing by Rakei Te Kura	82
7.2	Sarah's drawing of the smiling dinosaur	87
7.3	Sarah's drawing of the witch's hat	87
8.1	Whakamana/empowerment	92
8.2	A reification of paki ako and learning stories	95
8.3	A third way forward for creative capacity building: Children and tamariki as Kaitiaki/Trustees for animating the objects in the museums	99
8.4	Tumbling tetrahedron, or "folded" triangle	105

Rethinking Education: Series Editor Foreword

Education is the way a society produces its own future. But what sort of future is this? For more than three centuries, in the Western world, it's been wedded to an ideal of progress. A progressive education, according to its advocates, makes it possible for advances in human knowledge, forged by bringing the powers of the intellect to bear upon the material of empirical observation, to be passed from one generation to the next. Thanks to education, they insist, each generation can stand upon the shoulders of its forbears, contributing thereby to the ascent of civilisation as a whole. Empowered by the voice of reason, the educated are authorised to speak on behalf of a world whose sheer factuality subtends the vagaries of human experience. Here, in the community of reason, everyone is interchangeable. Problems have their right answers, and it makes no difference who comes up with them.

But what if the dream of progress turns out to be a chimaera? What if our much-vaunted civilisation is but a castle in the air, that leaves behind a world in ruins? Has progress, in its mission to wipe out the difference, and to measure the achievements of every generation by a universal standard, been achieved at the expense of human flourishing, and more than that, of the flourishing of all forms of life? Is it too much to dream of another sort of future, not of progress but of renewal—a future that would afford room for everyone and everything to thrive in this wondrous planet we all share, both presently and forever? For in this, surely, lies the proper meaning of sustainability. Whereas progressivists imagine every generation as a layer, each adding to the one before, in an education for sustainability generations would not so much be stacked vertically as wound longitudinally, like the overlapping fibres of a rope. It would be in their very overlap that the work of education is carried on.

Could this be what education is really about: learning to live together in difference? The very word education, after all, comes from the Latin *ex-* ("out") plus *ducere* ("to lead"). Education literally leads us out into the world. And as a way of leading out, it is fundamentally a practice of exposure. Its purpose is not to arm ourselves with knowledge, or to shore up our defences so that we can better cope with adversity. It is rather to disarm, to relinquish the security of established standpoints and positions, and by the same token, to attend more closely to the world around us and respond to what we find there with skill and sensitivity. Its primary commitment, in short, is to the fostering not of rationality but response-ability. If the voice of reason belongs at once to everyone and no one, with response-ability every voice is different, yet as in a choir or conversation, it comes forth only through its participation with the voices of others.

This kind of education doesn't separate knowledge from life but joins with the very forces of life—forces that create idea and ways of experiencing the world—in its ongoing fashioning. In their education, teachers and students embark together on a journey that may be difficult, even uncomfortable, with no certain outcome. This calls for care, patience and a willingness to experiment. Nevertheless, the journey is one in which generations can collaborate in finding a way into the future. It is not, then, for teachers to transmit knowledge readymade. Their task is rather to set an example, to serve as constant companions for their students and tireless critics of their work. And it is for students to follow in their footsteps while improvising a passage for themselves.

In the face of the still-dominant model of progressive education, the volumes in this series explore ways of thinking education otherwise—ways that give hope for coming generations and for the renewal of life. They offer visions for the future, manifestos, experimental curricula, speculative syllabi and case studies of alternative education at work. In line with Routledge's *Focus* series, they are short and provocative, intended for academics, researchers, professionals and students alike. We hope these volumes will convince our readers that other ways are possible!

The Editors

Acknowledgements

We acknowledge with thanks the Marsden Fund grant for this project from the Royal Society of New Zealand—Te Apārangi. We also acknowledge the contributions to this book by the teachers and kaiako; these contributions illustrate pedagogies of care and creative capacity building in numerous ways, and we thank them all.

1 Culture, Context and Creativity

> Part of what makes cultural institutions like museums powerful forums for the creation of imagined communities is the fact that they are potentially ideal public spaces where personal, private or autobiographical narratives come into contact with larger-scale, collective or national narratives in mutually inter-animating ways.
> (Rowe et al., 2002, p. 98)

> Relationships between people and the natural environment, between tangible and intangible dimensions, between organic and inorganic material, and between past and future constitute the foundations upon which indigenous populations understand the world. An energy flow that spirals outwards connects the multiple threads so that even very small objects become part of a wider context that gives them shape and meaning.
> (Durie, 2010, p. 239)

The quotes that begin this chapter introduce a framing in this book about culture, context and creativity when teachers and young children visit treasured objects in museums (widely defined). Shawn Rowe, James Wertsch and Tatyana Kosyaeva emphasise one feature of a creative response: "Linking Little (personal) Narratives to Big Ones" in history museums, and, in a very different context—indigenous Māori in Aotearoa New Zealand—Mason Durie describes a cultural ecosystem in which very small become "part of a wider context that gives them shape and meaning". These framings provided some ideas for describing a way forward for the explorations of children's creative capacity building. In this chapter, we begin with culture, introduce two early years' education contexts, and introduce a well-researched and revisited topic, creativity.

DOI: 10.4324/9781003313601-1

2 *Culture, Context and Creativity*

Culture: A bicultural project, creating spaces for dialogue across difference

Linda Tuhiwai Smith, a professor at the University of Waikato in Aotearoa New Zealand, commented in 2008 that bicultural research is "on tricky ground: indigenous researchers are committed to a platform for changing the status quo and see the engagement by indigenous researchers as an important lever for transforming institutions, communities and society" (2008, p. 119). She suggests, too, that *qualitative* research is an important tool for indigenous communities: it seems, she says, to be most able "to weave and unravel competing storylines: ..." and "to create spaces for dialogue across difference" (p. 136). Some of those different cultural storylines in Aotearoa New Zealand are signalled in the reference to an 1840 Treaty between Māori and Pākehā (non-Māori) in the national early childhood curriculum:

> Te Tiriti o Waitangi (The Treaty of Waitangi) is New Zealand's founding document. Signed in 1840 by representatives of Māori and the Crown, this agreement provided the foundation upon which Māori and Pākehā (non-Māori) would build their relationship as citizens of Aotearoa New Zealand. Central to this relationship was a commitment to live together in a spirit of partnership and the acceptance of obligations for participation and protection.
> (Ministry of Education, 2017, p. 3)

This book is a volume in the Routledge series on Anthropology and/as Education. Our discussions might be described as education and/as anthropology, as we explore comparisons of creative capacity building in education across these two different cultural sites. At both sites, it was impossible to disentangle the curriculum-in-practice and participant observing. At Mana Tamariki, Brenda and Leanne were both kaiako (teachers) for the four- and five-year-olds, and this included their usual way of documenting the children's learning over time in story format. At Tai Tamariki, Margaret and Jeanette, both of them qualified early childhood teachers before becoming university academics, were also participating observers, documenting this creative capacities' topic, and occasionally taking on the role of teachers. They also took photographs that ended up in the children's portfolios, and they informally interviewed the early childhood teachers at the early childhood centre. These two different linguistic and cultural environments are central to our discussions throughout the book.

Cultural contexts: Two early childhood centres in Aotearoa New Zealand

The descriptions and encounters in this book span two early years education sites. The first site is Mana Tamariki kōhanga (early childhood centre) and kura (school) in the same building. *Ki tā te Māori titiro, ki tā te wairua Māori* (where the perspective is Māori, the Māori spirit is engaged; see also the quote from Professor Mason Durie at the beginning of the chapter).

The second is Tai Tamariki kindergarten (*pākehā* and *tauiwi*, where English is mostly spoken and diverse cultural contexts and viewpoints are included).

Mana tamariki kōhanga and kura

The very first Kōhanga Reo in Aotearoa New Zealand, a total immersion Māori language nest for children aged 0–5 years, was established in 1982. It was followed in 1985 by the launch of Kura Kaupapa Māori (total immersion Māori Primary Schools), followed in 1993 by Wharekura (total immersion Māori language secondary schools). An urban Māori educational setting, Mana Tamariki seeks to support families who are committed to the regeneration of the Māori language and culture in the home by providing an educational pathway for children to learn in a particular way that gives priority to the language and culture. Early on, the Māori team from Mana Tamariki gifted a title to this project: *He taonga, he rerenga arorangi*. They explain as follows:

> *He taonga, he rerenga arorangi* is the Māori title of our Royal Society of New Zealand Marsden Fund research project. It is not a direct translation of the English title Young children in museums: Creative capacity building. In the context of this research, *he taonga* (treasured objects) are broadly defined. The second part of the title, *he rerenga arorangi*, is taken from the Māori text of Te Whāriki where *arorangi* is defined as 'unrestricted'. The word *rerenga* expresses movement. So here, *rerenga arorangi* relates to the freedom to soar unrestricted to the heights of one's creative potential to a space where the spirit is nurtured. The title becomes: 'Where there are treasured objects, the spirit is nurtured and creativity will be inspired'.

As a Māori language immersion educational setting, kaiako in Te Kōhanga Reo and Te Kura Kaupapa Māori o Mana Tamariki had already carried out visits to their nearby Te Manawa museum and other sites in the landscape in accordance with tikanga Māori

4 *Culture, Context and Creativity*

(cultural protocols). In order to adhere to cultural requirements kaiako ensured that children were thoroughly prepared through pre-visit conversations and wānanga (meetings). Children with tribal connections to the taonga (treasures of cultural value) were encouraged to carry their role as tangata whenua (hosts) by leading karakia and mihi (acknowledgements and greetings) and physically leading the group into the exhibition spaces. Each visit included for kaiako and tamariki a process of pre-visit, visit and post-visit that was planned and purposeful.

Earlier research at Mana Tamariki[1]

Mana Tamariki had a history of collaboration with universities. An earlier project was to research the cultural protocols for establishing a Māori garden (Soutar et al., 2010, pp. 35–40).[2] Funding was won from a Ministry of Education "Centres of Innovation programme", designed to fund innovative projects in early childhood centres for three years, supported by research associates of their choice. Mana Tamariki developed a metaphor for their two chosen researchers (University of Waikato professors Te Wharehuia Milroy and Margaret Carr) that nicely defines advice for external researchers whose role it is to support local teachers to achieve their own aspirations:

> Our research associates were given the title of Pou Turuturu by Mana Tamariki, a name we selected to reflect their role. Turuturu are stakes used by weavers to hang garments, freeing the weaver's hands and thus enabling her or him to concentrate on the work. In this analogy, the Mana Tamariki whānau is the weaver, the research is the garment and the two Pou Turuturu are the stakes upon which the weaving hangs until it is completed, at which time the turuturu are released.
> (Brenda Soutar with Te Whānau o Mana Tamariki, 2010, p. 37)

That earlier project was built on the notion of *te tamaiti hei raukura*—the child as a high achiever who exemplifies the hopes and aspirations of their people—and included visits to the local museum, Te Manawa, within walking distance of the Mana Tamariki kōhanga and kura. The museum was not previously viewed as a place of research but more as a place to visit and observe. Brenda had commented that museums are one of several community places where space is made outside of te ao Māori (the Māori world) for people to engage with te ao Māori; they are places where

Culture, Context and Creativity 5

we can honour the past and engage children with their ancestors' legacy to assist their resiliency as Māori. Mana Tamariki's examples expanded the notion of a "museum". The tamariki and kaiako (children and teachers from the kōhanga and kura) visited their local marae, ngahere (native bush), and the local Manawatu gorge and river; all of these as authentic settings for taonga (treasures of cultural value). A publication entitled *Growing Raukura* written by Brenda Soutar and Te Whānau o Mana Tamariki (2010)[3] described this experience of developing an indigenous garden, with authoritative cultural advice and assistance from Professor Te Wharehuia Milroy. It includes his comments about the commitments that had been made, adding that "the tamariki will be the inheritors of this knowledge and wisdom" (op. cit., p. 40).

We have built on that earlier research, especially borrowing the value of using triangles to describe some of the cultural complexity; we elaborate on this in Chapter 2.

Tai Tamariki Kindergarten

The second site is Tai Tamariki Kindergarten where English is the language mostly spoken. Tai Tamariki Kindergarten (translated as "Children of the Tide") was opened in 2010 on the ground floor of Te Papa Tongawera Museum of New Zealand (commonly referred to as "Te Papa") in Wellington, the capital city of Aotearoa New Zealand. The kindergarten is a full-day, education-and-care, early childhood centre for children aged three months to five years. It was established in response to ongoing requests from employees at Te Papa to have a childcare facility because of an acute shortage of childcare in the inner city; it was also available to other families who live or work in the central city. A Kindergarten Association, responsible for the governance and management of a large number of kindergartens in the region, entered an agreement with the museum management to provide the early childhood centre on the premises of the museum. A Heads of Agreement between the two parties outlined their vision to nurture "life-long learners, providing children, their parents and whānau and the staff who are part of it (the kindergarten) with transformative experiences in a rich cultural context" (Museum of New Zealand Te Papa Tongarewa & Wellington Region Free Kindergarten Association, 2009, p. 1).

Earlier research at Tai Tamariki

When Tai Tamariki Kindergarten was established, the CEO of Te Papa supported the view that this early childhood centre would be a site for research. A group of University of Waikato researchers led by Jeanette Clarkin-Phillips collaborated with the teachers and the Kindergarten Association management to win funding for a project to research the Tai Tamariki children's responses to exhibitions held "upstairs" in the museum. They explored the learning about indigenous cultural values and protocols that occurred for the three- and four-year-olds, and the teachers, during and after visits to an exhibition entitled *Kahu Ora: Living Cloaks*, a collection of Māori kākahu (traditional cloaks) woven from harakeke (native flax). The exhibition included a studio where weavers were engaged in the complex task of preparing the harakeke and weaving the intricate designs to tell specific stories. On their visits to see the exhibition, the children were able to view the kākahu, watch the weavers and gain other information from the digital resources at the exhibition. The weavers gave the children explanations of the weaving and of the cultural protocols that accompanied them. Back at the kindergarten, three kākahu were constructed collaboratively by several children. They were supported by their new knowledge, and they added their own materials, patterns and symbols in imaginative, creative ways. For instance, as one child weaver explained on her label for the museum exhibition, the feathers on her cloak came from feather dusters. Then, there was great excitement when the interpreter of the exhibition decided to invite the children to exhibit their kākahu in the main *Kahu Ora* exhibition.

> The kākahu on loan from the kindergarten were accorded the same rituals and protocols as the other korowai at the exhibition. This included a blessing by a Māori elder and the careful boxing, transporting and displaying of the kākahu, and labelling each in the same way as the 'official' exhibits: with children dictating comments.
> (Clarkin-Phillips et al., 2014, p. 4)

One of the Māori teachers at the kindergarten taught the children a karakia (an acknowledgement, in this case, "to give thanks to our ancestors for our treasures").

A bicultural early childhood curriculum includes creative opportunities

This was a bicultural project. Anna Craft (2005, p. 100) had always reminded us of creativity's plural nature, specifically that creativity and how it might be fostered *are not culture-blind*. At the beginning of an edited book entitled, *Creativity, Wisdom and Trusteeship*, she adds (our italics):

However—and here we come to the questions at the forefront of this book—if we are asking how we use our creativity wisely, and who are the trustees of generative thought in a globalized world in the early 21st century, *we could perhaps question the appropriateness of fostering creativity as if we were culture-blind*, that is, in a way which implies the imposition of one cultural model on another.

(Craft et al., 2008, p. 23)

The pedagogy in both early childhood centres, including when teachers were visiting museums, followed a bicultural and bilingual early childhood curriculum, Te Whāriki (Ministry of Education, 2017, pp. 24–25). The title "Te Whāriki" is a "weaving": "A whāriki that empowers the child and carries our aspirations" (p. 10). We could propose that some of the 20 Learning Outcomes, described as "knowledge, skills, attitudes and dispositions" in five curricula "strands", might be linked to a creativity agenda. In 1996, when Te Whāriki was first developed, each principle and strand was given dual Māori and English names. These broad titles remain unchanged in the 2017 version. The principles are as follows (pp. 18–21):

Empowerment | Whakamana
Holistic Development | Kotahitanga
Family and Community | Whānau Tangata
Relationships | Ngā Hononga

We note that any translations from te reo Māori into the English language—in the learning outcomes that follow here, and in this book—do not mean "equals"; they are always deemed to be approximate because of cultural differences. Here, we have included some of the learning outcomes that might be relevant to the building of the creative capacity building.

Mana atua	**Well-being**
Te whakahua whakairo	Expressing their feelings
Mana whenua	**Belonging**
Te waihanga hononga	Making connections between people, places and things in their world
Te marama ki te ahua o nga whakahaere me te mohio ki te panoni	Understanding how things work here and adapting to change

(*Continued*)

8 Culture, Context and Creativity

Te mahi whakaute	Showing respect for kaupapa, rules and rights of others
Mana tangata	**Contribution**
Ta ngākau makura	Treating others fairly and including them in play
Te ngākau aroha	Using a range of strategies to play and learn
Mana reo	**Communication/language**
He kōrero ā-waha	Understanding oral language (any method of communication) and using it for a range of purposes
He kōrero paki	Enjoying hearing (includes watching) stories and retelling and creating them
He kōrero auaha	Expressing their feelings and ideas using a wide range of materials and modes
Mana aotūroa	**Exploration**
Te whakaaro me te tūhurahura i te pūtaiao	Playing, imagining, inventing and experimenting
Te wero a-tinana	Moving confidently and challenging themselves
Te hiraurau hopanga	Using a range of strategies for reasoning and problem solving
Te rangahau me te mātauranga	Making sense of their worlds by generating and refining working theories

From little to big: An ecosocial framing

The comments by Shawn M. Rowe, James V. Wertsch, Tatyana Kosyaeva and Mason Durie at the beginning of this chapter reflect our decision to consider the observations and conversations during the visits as an ecosocial framing that uniquely encouraged and defined contexts for creative thinking. Further comments by Rowe et al. (2002) also resonated with our experience—and the observations of the other accompanying early childhood teachers as well:

> It turns out that some of the encounters between little and big narratives that are most interesting from our perspective can be some of the most frustrating to those who organize museum exhibits. From their perspective, visitors' discussions about how their lives are tied to an exhibit often reflect a failure to engage

with the exhibit in the 'proper' way. However, just what constitutes the 'proper' way to engage with an exhibit may be a point of contention within the museum itself (p. 98).

Ecosocial frames also reflect the kaiako's everyday pedagogy and their relationships with tamariki and whānau (families), as well as when they are visiting museums. Jay L. Lemke (2000) comments on this:

> Meanings are not made by organisms but by persons, and they are not made within organisms but within an ecosocial system that minimally includes other persons and the things they make meaning about and that minimally operates over timescales sufficient for a developing person to come to engage in socially meaningful interactions with others and with the nonhuman surround (p. 283).

Tim Ingold (2018, p. 49) writes that *objects* of regard become animate *things* when they "act, they speak to us directly, make us think: not just about them, but with them. They become part of our world, and we of theirs". From an Aotearoa New Zealand context, Professor Mason Durie (2010, pp. 243–244) writes that "indigeneity is about people and their natural environments growing older together. Relationships in time are as important as spatial relationships, and the ecological perspective, which underlines indigenous world views, places emphasis on both past and future relationships".

Creative capacities: An interest in attitudes

As we came to recognise the *animating* that Ingold and Durie describe, we began to unpack the role of culture and context, focusing especially on the ways in which the teachers—and the children in these encounters—saw their encounters with taonga (in the museums: treasures and objects of interest and, usually, of cultural value) as opportunities to introduce creative perspectives and storying.

We began to focus especially on the ways in which the teachers, and the children, saw their encounters with taonga as opportunities to introduce creative perspectives and storying. We interpret this as an interest in "attitudes", rather than knowledge only. This alternative is documented from way back; in his 1938 book *Experience and Education*, John Dewey wrote:

> Perhaps the greatest of all pedagogical fallacies is the notion that a person learns only the particular thing he is studying at the time.

Collateral learning in the way of formation of enduring attitudes, of likes and dislikes, may be and often is much more important than the spelling lesson or lesson in geography or history that is learned. For these attitudes are fundamentally what count in the future. The most important attitude that can be formed is that of desire to go on learning (p. 49).

In this book, we explore how these museum visits might not only continue a desire to go on learning, to be curious and to be knowledgeable, but also to provide opportunities to hone creative attitudes and capacities. Mihaly Csikszentmihalyi, for instance, in his key 1996 book entitled *Creativity* (p. 346) suggested that "the first step" toward a more creative life is the cultivation of the attitudes of curiosity and interest. We turn to the national early childhood curriculum in Aotearoa New Zealand, *Te Whāriki*, where learning is emphasised (Ministry of Education, 2017, p. 7) as "knowledge, skills, attitudes and dispositions that support lifelong learning". While Dewey called them "enduring attitudes", the education research literature has provided a number of suggestions: *thinking dispositions* (Perkins et al., 1993: being ready willing and able); *habits of mind* (Costa & Kallick, 2000), *mindset* (Dweck, 2006), and *key competencies* (Rychen & Salganik, 2003). The notion that being curious can be a disposition, a habit of mind, or a mindset is significant for our discussions about *collaborative* encounters: the children might have the ability or skill to be curious in some contexts, but may not be ready or willing to display (and therefore to practise and develop) a questioning capacity in a museum visit. This, one might think, could be especially true in an exhibit of large-as-life dinosaurs in *Tyrannosaurs: Meet the Family* at The Museum of New Zealand Te Papa Tongarewa. This was advertised in the museum's "Education Resource for Teachers" as "an immersive multimedia experience that explores how these tyrannical dinosaurs, with their massive skulls, powerful jaws, and bone-crunching teeth, became the world's top predators".

So we have been exploring questions about the building of creative *capacities*, choosing museum visits as a rich context to explore how these educational encounters can, might and/or do become creative capacity-building sites; and we noted how the combination of children, teachers and taonga/things in the museum worked together. We will explore, with Tim Ingold (2018, p. 49), the notion that the children and the teachers were regarding the taonga/things "not as *objects* of regard but as animate things in their own right". These were sociocultural and ecosocial questions. In this book, the cultural and social ecology

Culture, Context and Creativity 11

framing extends our discussions further, beyond the museum encounter. The two quotes that begin the chapter also reflect this thinking.

Writing about anthropology and anthropologists and storying, Jerome Bruner comments:

> Indeed, the images and stories that we provide for guidance to speakers with respect to when they may speak and what they may say in what situations may indeed be a first constraint on the nature of selfhood. It may be one of the many reasons why anthropologists (in contrast to psychologists) have always been attentive not only to the content but to the form of the myths and stories they encounter among their 'subjects'.
>
> For stories define the range of canonical characters, the settings in which they operate, the actions that are permissible and comprehensible. And thereby they provide, so to speak, a map of possible roles and possible worlds in which action, thought and self-definition are permissible (or desirable).
> (Bruner, J. Chapter 4: The Transactional Self in Bruner & Haste, 1987, p. 91)

Problem finding and problem solving: Mapping possible roles and possible worlds

Also valuable for our interpretations was the discussion in J. W. Getzels and M. Csikszentmihalyi (1975)'s chapter entitled *From Problem Solving to Problem Finding*. They begin their commentary with a question:

> How did we come to study the creativity of *problems* when we began by studying the creativity of *solutions*? How did we reach the conclusion that the creative act involves problem finding as much as it does problem solving (if the two processes can be separated at all), and to hold the hypothesis that creative problems may be as fruitful a subject of study as creative solutions? (p. 90)

They explain:

> As Einstein put the issue with regard to science, "The formulation of a problem is often more essential than its solution, which may be merely a matter of mathematical or experimental skill" (p. 92).

Anna Craft (2005) has also pursued this idea, expanding on her argument that: "The thesis is that possibility thinking involves a continuum of strategies, with at one end the question 'What does this do?' to 'What can I do with this?', both of which have the potential to encompass both problem finding and problem solving" (p. 36). Writing in 2013 she also sounds a warning, commenting on international pressures toward a classroom as "a marketized and positivist world of measurement, comparison and competition, where certainties are provided by progress harnessed to acquisition" (Craft, 2013, p. 130). She adds:

> This [positivist] place does not necessarily acknowledge the multiple ways in which young people are also expert and empowered, and the many ways in which exciting, meaningful and high quality learning may occur between peers, across ages, between experts and novices, harnessing curiosity and stimulating co-creativity.

In his book, *Making Stories,* Jerome Bruner (2002) also writes: "Through narrative, we construct, reconstruct, in some ways reinvent yesterday and tomorrow. *Memory and imagination fuse in the process*" (p. 93, our emphasis). Of course, memory plus imagination *might* "fuse in the process"; however, interactions that are "fused" in drawings and/or photographs, and/or written up by kaiako as stories in a child's portfolio will record some of the ways in which children are expert, empowered and creative by "making material" the examples and storylines of creative capacity building. They construct narratives that tamariki/children, kaiako/teachers and whānau/families can revisit, time and time again. Here are two examples, recorded before our observations began. In Chapter 2, we will introduce this process as *a reifying* (making material), in Cultural Anchor 3.

Two examples of creative encounters

Example 1: Imagining a new kupu (word) for an English artefact[4]

A group of tamariki from the Mana Tamariki kōhanga are visiting an exhibition at Te Manawa, the local museum; the kaiako and the tamariki speak in te reo Māori. The exhibition includes a model English sailing ship; the word for this in English is not readily available in te reo Māori. This is compounded by the fact that the exhibition does not connect this artefact with Māori history (i.e., as a similar ship to the one that brought Captain James Cook to Aotearoa in 1769). Five-year-old Rakei Te Kura is curious; he notices the rudder, and asks the kaiako,

Leanne, what it is for; she answers, and admits that she is uncertain about the name for the artefact in te reo Māori. After thinking about the problem for a minute or two, Rakei Te Kura finds a solution:

Rakei Te Kura: Mōhio au te ingoa o tēnei	Oh, now I know a name for this!
Kaiako: He aha?	What is it?
Rakei Te Kura: He ikarere! Āe, ka pēra me he ika.	A swimming fish! Yes, because it moves like a fish. [ika = fish, rere = swim/run]
Kaiako: Tēnā koe, e whakaae ana au ki tēnā! He ikarere.	That's right! Thank you for that. I agree with you on that! It's an "ikarere".

There are a number of features in this short episode that can be linked to ideas about creativity and creative encounters. It reflects our development of a *definition of creativity*: a going beyond prior information or knowledge to add a restorying. Rakei te Kura was responding to Leanne's *puzzlement*: a question of linguistics, of te reo Māori in a context which was in English. He recognised a problem to be solved, and he called on his prior knowledge of how language is constructed in te reo Māori to propose a word for his teacher's consideration, using an imaginative metaphor (a swimming fish) developed from his observation of and conversation with Leanne about the rudder. His inclination to "reconstruct and reinvent" (Bruner's definition of narrative) created a space for dialogue: Leanne then wrote a paki ako (learning story)[5] in te reo Māori of this conversation for Rakei Te Kura's portfolio, commenting with admiration and making this explicit as an example of *e waihanga ana* [imagination]. She also explains that she checked the Māori dictionary and discovered that there was already a kupu (word) in te reo Māori for a rudder, and she included it in the learning story. Adding this example to all the children's portfolios (the tradition at Mana Tamariki) enacts the curriculum principle of *whakamana* (every child will experience an empowering curriculum that recognises and enhances their mana[6] and supports them to enhance the mana—prestige/integrity/authority—of others). The message that this capacity for imagination is valued will be carried forward by the narrative account. Chapter 4 has more to say about imagination and creativity.

Example 2: The defining of a creative process was integral to the pedagogy

One of the kaiako at Tai Tamariki kindergarten (the mostly English language site) documented her work during a collaborative episode with a group of three- and four-year-olds. Although it is only slightly linked to a specific museum visit (a dinosaur is briefly mentioned), it is about the kaiako, Maiangi, encouraging the tamariki to build their creative capacities and storying during rehearsals towards a theatre production for the other children. The children had raided the "dress-up" box to develop a cast of self-chosen characters who will all take their turn "on stage". They include characters adapted from their cultural lexicon of well-known fantasy stories: Peter Pan, Robin Hood, a Wolf (Robin Hood's pet), Butterflies, Fairies, and Treasure. Maiangi noted, in her documentation of this story for the children's portfolios, that "There are a lot of opportunities for dancing". She also commented as follows: "I was trying to explain to them that it's good when there's something.... some tension, something goes wrong". Four-year-old Ted (who plays Robin Hood) says "OK, the Wolf (Jack) used to be my pet and he turned Bad!". And I was saying "That's exactly what I'm talking about. Like a twist or something like that". She writes the script for the play for each of the actor's portfolios. It includes the following:

> Robin Hood says: "I'll lead you to where it (the Treasure) is, but in the forest there's a bad wolf—he used to be my pet but he turned bad ... he might eat us!"
>
> Then Bad Wolf (Jack) jumps out "RRRaaaagh!" Then all the Butterflies and Fairies and Peter Pan and Everyone said "Abracadabra!" and he changed into a pet dinosaur....
>
> Then everyone kept searching for the treasure and when it was found they shared it all around and were very happy! Then they had another big dance! The End.

One point of interest here, for us, was "Who was responsible for the storying?". It was, we suggest, a combination of the children, the materials available to indicate the characters—vital for the story-line—and Maiangi (the teacher) who provided the instruction that a "good" story needs to have a "twist", in this case, the inclusion of surprise or a problem (a Bad Wolf) to be solved. The problem of a Bad Wolf in the story is solved by the useful device of a magical and collaborative "Abracadabra". We will explore the role of surprise and uncertainty, as a pedagogy for creative capacity encounters, in Chapter 5.

In both these examples, a problem to be solved is central to the collaboration. The Mana Tamariki story began with a problem-finding introduced by the teacher and the problem solving was taken on as a responsibility by five-year-old Rakei Te Kura: the search for a word in te reo Māori. The problem in the Tai Tamariki story was also introduced by the teacher, Maiangi, and taken on as a responsibility by four-year-old Ted. Jerome Bruner provides a label for these problems: Trouble. In his book entitled "*Making Stories*", Bruner (2002, p. 28) suggests that plans often go awry; he quotes the poet Robert Burns: "the best laid plans ... gang aft aglea" and makes the optimistic comment that "thanks to the regularizing power of culture, our plans usually work out quite quietly and well". He then adds a comment about the power of story: "But it is our narrative gift that gives us the power to make sense of things when they don't". Each of these examples of "making sense" and problem solving, relied on cultural memory or knowledge: Rakei Te Kura's knowledge of the structure of many words in te reo Māori, and Ted's knowledge of English fairy tales and (prompted by the teacher) an understanding that storylines in these stories commonly begin with a problem and then end with a heroic solution (Little Red Riding Hood and her encounter with the Wolf in the English lexicon might have come to Ted's mind).

Notes

1 Some of the earlier research has also been described in a paper published in the journal *Children's Geographies* (Carr et al., 2018).
2 In that context, "Raukura" are high achievers who exemplify the hopes and aspirations of their people: "hei raukura mo tona iwi" (Mataira, 1987 as cited in Soutar et al., 2010).
3 Whānau in this context includes the tamariki (children), kaiako (teachers) and whānau [extended families of the tamariki].
4 This example has already been published in *Children's Geographies* (Carr et al., 2018).
5 *Learning stories* and *paki ako* are narrative methods of assessment, commonly used in early childhood settings in Aotearoa New Zealand, see Carr and Lee (2012, 2019). A section entitled "Assessment, planning and evaluation" in the national early childhood curriculum (Ministry of Education, 2017, p. 63) includes the following statement: "Portfolios may include annotated photographs, children's art, recordings or transcripts of oral language, kaiako observations and learning stories".
6 *Mana* is impossible to define in English. Te Whāriki, the 2017 national early childhood curriculum includes Principle 1 entitled "Empowerment | Whakamana". It explains (p. 18): "This principle means that every child will experience an empowering curriculum that recognises and enhances their mana and supports them to enhance the mana of others. Viewed from a Māori perspective, all children are born with mana inherited from their tipuna (ancestors). Mana is the power of being and must be upheld and enhanced".

References

Bruner, J. (2002). *Making stories: Law, literature, life.* Harvard University Press.
Bruner, J., & Haste, H. (Eds.). (1987). *Making sense: The child's construction of the world.* Routledge.
Carr, M., Clarkin-Phillips, J., Soutar, B., Clayton, L., Wipaki, M., Wipaki-Hawkins, R., Cowie, B., & Gardner, S. (2018). Young children visiting museums: Exhibits, children and teachers co-author the journey. *Children's Geographies, 16*(5), 558–570. 10.1080/14733285.2018.1480750
Carr, M., & Lee, W. (2012). *Learning stories: Constructing learner identities in early education.* Sage.
Carr, M., & Lee, W. (2019). *Learning stories in practice.* Sage.
Clarkin-Phillips, J., Carr, M., Thomas, R., O'Brien, C., Crowe, N., & Armstrong, G. (2014). Children as teachers in a museum: Growing their knowledge of an indigenous culture. *The International Journal of the Inclusive Museum, 6*(4), 1–11.
Costa, A.L., & Kallick, B. (Eds). (2000). *Habits of mind: A developmental series.* Four volumes: Discovering and exploring (Book 1), Activating and engaging (Book 2), Assessing and reporting (Book 3), Integrating and sustaining (Book 4). Association for Supervision and Curriculum.
Craft, A. (2005). *Creativity in schools: Tensions and dilemmas.* Routledge.
Craft, A. (2013). Childhood, possibility thinking and wise, humanising educational futures. *International Journal of Educational Research, 61,* 126–134.
Craft, A., Gardner, H., & Claxton, G. (Eds.). (2008). *Creativity, wisdom, and trusteeship: Exploring the role of trusteeship.* Corwin Press.
Csikszentmihalyi, M. (1996). *Creativity: Flow and the psychology of discovery and invention.* HarperCollins.
Dewey, J. (1938). *Experience and education.* The Macmillan Company.
Durie, M. (2010). Outstanding universal value: How relevant is indigeneity? In R. Selby, P. Moore & M. Mulholland (Eds.), *Māori and the environment: Kaitiaki* (pp. 239, 241, 243). Huia.
Dweck, C. S. (2006). *Mindset: The new psychology of success.* Random House.
Getzels, J. W., & Csikszentmihalyi, M. (1975). From problem solving to problem finding. In I. A. Taylor & J. W. Getzels (Eds.), *Perspectives in creativity* (pp. 90–116). Aldine Publishing.
Ingold, T. (2018). *Anthropology and/as education.* Routledge.
Lemke, J. L. (2000). Across the scales of time: Artifacts, activities, and meanings in ecosocial systems. *Mind, Culture, and Activity, 7*(4), 273–290. 10.1207/S15327884MCA0704_03
Ministry of Education. (2017). *Te Whāriki.* https://www.education.govt.nz/assets/Documents/Early-Childhood/Te-Whariki-Early-Childhood-Curriculum-ENG-Web.pdf
Museum of New Zealand Te Papa Tongarewa & Wellington Region Free Kindergarten Association. (2009). *Memorandum of Understanding.*
Perkins, D. N., Jay, E., & Tishman, S. (1993). Beyond abilities: A dispositional theory of thinking. *Merrill-Palmer Quarterly, 39*(1), 1–21.

Rowe, S. M., Wertsch, J. V., & Kosyaeva, T. Y. (2002). Linking little narratives to big ones: Narrative and public memory in history museums. *Culture & Psychology*, 8(1), 96–112. 10.1177/1354067X02008001621

Rychen, D. S., & Salganik, L. H. (Eds.). (2003). *Key competencies for a successful life and a well-functioning society*. Hagrefe & Huber.

Soutar, B., with Te Whanau o Mana Tamariki. (2010). Growing raukura. In A. Meade (Ed.), *Dispersing the waves: Innovation in early childhood education* (pp. 35–40). NZCER Press.

Tuhiwai Smith, T. (2008). On tricky ground: Researching the native in the age of uncertainty. In N. K. Denzin & Y. S. Lincoln (Eds.), *The landscape of qualitative research* (pp. 113–143). Sage.

2 Thinking in Triangles

> In the case of the research pattern the triangle acts as a critical pattern for the triangulation of the contributing threads that entwine the circle representing te reo [language] as the house of cultural sustainability.
> (Professor Robert Jahnke [personal communication November 2007] writing for an earlier research project at Mana Tamariki)

> For Dewey the meaning of the world is, after all, not located in the things and events themselves, but in the social practices in which things, gestures, sounds and events play a role. We could therefore say that because meanings only exist *in* social practices, it is, in a sense, located *in-between* those who constitute the social practice through their interactions.
> Gert J.J. Biesta (2013, p. 31)

In an earlier, traditional garden project at Mana Tamariki described in Chapter 1, communications from two Māori professors (Te Wharehuia Milroy from the University of Waikato and Robert Jahnke from Massey University) contributed explanations of the *triangle* as a metaphor that could inspire that (2008–2009) garden research project—and therefore, we thought, other research projects too.

Both those Māori kaumatua and scholars commented on the conceptual power of the tapatoru, the triangle, in Māori tradition. During that garden project, Te Wharehuia Milroy explained to Brenda that there were countless examples of the importance of the triangle in te ao Māori. He gave two illustrations:

1 *Te Kawau Māro*: This term relates to the flight of the kawau [cormorant or shag] where the birds fly in the formation of a triangle. The leader sets the pace and guides the direction of the group with the full force of the others behind. This formation was

DOI: 10.4324/9781003313601-2

imitated by the taua [war party] as it was considered an efficient way to advance into battle. If the formation is turned upside down, advancing becomes much more difficult with the minority behind encouraging the majority forward. Also, there would be too many navigators and directors.

2   *The shape of waka* [sea-going canoes]: Te Wharehuia explained that the ihu [prow] of the waka was shaped triangularly. This allowed the waka to more easily break through the waves. He explained the value of the triangle for research, using two whakataukī [proverbs] that emphasised the value of the triangle for problem solving.

"Ma te ihu o te waka e wāhi te ngaru" (The prow of the canoe will break through the waves).

"Kua whakaokaoka te ihu o te waka ngā ngaru" (The prow of the canoe has split open the wave).

Robert Jahnke (personal communication, 2007) further explained the significance of the triangle for research, using traditional weaving as a metaphor:

> More often than not ... the triangle is a critical element or building block that contributes to a number of taniko, raranga and whāriki patterns. One could argue that without the triangle unit the woven arts would be bereft of its rich vocabulary of meaning. In a further allegory, the aho [cross-threads] and whenu [lengthwise threads] combine to generate the triangle that in turn creates the significant patterns in the woven arts. Therefore, as a core composition of elements in the woven arts the triangle offers an appropriate symbol for binding together the threads of the weaving.

He adds, explaining the role of the triangle when the anchor (our word) is te reo, language:

> In the case of the research pattern the triangle acts as a critical pattern for the triangulation of the contributing threads that entwine the circle representing Te Reo as the house of cultural sustainability. In this case, the threads of the triangle become Children as Raukura[1], Learning Stories and Families.
> (Professor Jahnke, personal communication, November 2007)

In Chapter 1, we recognised that the task of writing about the creative capacity building was to also create spaces for dialogue across cultural differences. In this chapter, we outline four Cultural Anchors to do some of this work. Each triangle illustrates three dimensions for creative capacity building; as a cluster, they provide spaces for this book's dialogue across cultural differences, and we return to them in Chapters 7 and 8.

Cultural Anchors: Thinking from materials

Edwin Hutchins (2005), in a discussion of "material anchors for conceptual blends" argues for the central role of material objects in stabilising and strengthening reasoning processes. He stated: "From an anthropological perspective, I believe that the sorts of processes I describe here are absolutely essential to an understanding of the nature of human cognitive accomplishments" (p. 1562). He also explains and exemplifies "how the use of input spaces that contain material structure can create conceptual blends that permit people to do some *astonishing thinking*" (p. 1562, our italics). He used, as an example, early canoe navigators using the positioning of stars and islands as coordinates (p. 1567) for their "astonishing" feats of travel. Similarly, for the Aotearoa New Zealand context, Rangi Matamua, a professor at the University of Waikato, has provided a detailed account of the astronomy knowledge of early Māori explorers in his book *Matariki: Te Whetū Tapu o te Tau* (2017), in two versions: in te reo Māori and in English as "*Matariki: The Star of the Year*"). He comments, in the English version (p. 2):

> Astronomy was central in the populating of the islands of the Pacific. Polynesian explorers used the stars, among other techniques, to navigate their double-hulled canoes across the greatest expanse of water on the planet, to settle many islands, including Aotearoa. Māori used the stars to understand and interact with their environment, looking for the rising and setting of different points of light to tell them when to plant, when to harvest, when to hunt, when to fish, when to build, when to travel, when to celebrate and when to pray.

There is a metaphor for us here: a star cluster—he rerenga arorangi as coordinates for a space where the spirit is nurtured and creativity (astonishing thinking perhaps?) will be inspired. Each of our early years education communities is different, and in 1990, Jerome Bruner, a wise commentator on narrative and story reminded us that interpretations are always indeterminate: "For there are no causes to be grasped with certainty where the act of creating meaning is concerned, only acts, expressions, and contexts to be interpreted.... These contexts are always contexts of practice—asking what people are doing or trying to do in that context" (p. 118). Objects, Tim Ingold (2012, p. 437) argued, become animate *things* when they are "entangled in a skein of movement and affect" in the "web of life" of ecology. As a rough parallel, in our Cultural Anchor 1, objects become treasured taonga in a space where the spirit is nurtured (Figure 2.1).

So we constructed Cultural Anchors, as triangles, to anchor our discussions of "travelling" with the tamariki, kaiako and taonga during museum visits. They are explained and explored as follows. The first triangle deconstructs a title for our project, gifted to us all by the Māori team: *he taonga, he rerenga arorangi*. They explained and introduced it in Chapter 1, as follows:

> He taonga, he rerenga arorangi is the Māori title of our project. In the context of this research, *he taonga* (treasured artefacts) are broadly defined, The second part of the title, *he rerenga arorangi*, is taken from the Māori text of Te Whāriki [the New Zealand national early childhood curriculum] where *arorangi* is defined as unrestricted. The word *rerenga* expresses movement. So here, rerenga arorangi relates to the freedom to soar unrestricted to the heights of one's creative potential in a space where the spirit is nurtured.

Cultural Anchor 1

- He taonga, treasured material objects in museums (widely defined),
- he rerenga arorangi, soaring unrestricted to the heights of one's creative potential,
- he taonga, he rerenga arorangi: where there are treasured objects, the spirit is nurtured, and there is freedom to soar to the heights of one's creative potential.

Figure 2.1 Cultural Anchor 1.

He taonga, he rerenga arorangi is supported by *he taonga* and *arorangi*. We are writing about young children's and their teachers' encounters with taonga in museums, broadly defined, so taonga are the starting points for our discussions of creative capacity building.

In the example in Chapter 1, finding a word in te reo Māori, the pedagogy constructed the creative response: a genuine *uncertainty* expressed by the kaiako; combined with the *ambiguity* of the object this empowered the tamaiti [child] to be bold enough to imagine and suggest a solution. Finding appropriately Māori translations for new words in English is part of the kaupapa [philosophy and programme] at Mana Tamariki. In the Tai Tamariki story, the materials (the dress-ups) anchored the drama storyline; in that case, the pedagogy included a direct challenge to the children to construct a more creative and interesting storyline (one with a "twist") in a safe, collaborative and encouraging space (Figure 2.2).

Cultural Anchor 2

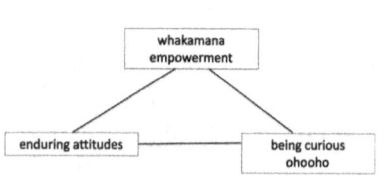

Figure 2.2 Cultural Anchor 2.

- Enduring attitudes and dispositions,
- being curious (e ohooho ana) (*Te Aho Matua*, Ministry of Education, 2008, p. 739),
- whakamana/empowerment (a curriculum principle in *Te Whāriki* (Ministry of Education, 2017, p. 21).

> Learning in the way of formation of enduring attitudes, of likes and dislikes, may be and often is much more important than the spelling lesson or lesson in geography or history that is learned. For these attitudes are fundamentally what count in the future.
>
> (Dewey, 1938, p. 49)

In this anchor's triangle, whakamana/empowerment, one of the early years' four curriculum principles (see Chapter 1) is supported by "being curious" as an "enduring attitude" (John Dewey's expression) or learning disposition. *Being curious* as a forerunner of "empowerment" implies that tamariki are ready and willing to ask questions, and, when the environment is supportive, are enabled to recognise or construct problems and to seek solutions in response to that curiosity. In Guy Claxton's words, writing about wisdom:

I prefer to think of dispositions rather than skills because wise actions will not be produced spontaneously unless a person is disposed towards them, that is, inclined to see appropriate occasions and to act on them. To be wise, I think you have to be ready and willing, as well as able (2008, p. 42).

Other literature on learning dispositions in education, especially the writing and research led by David Perkins during Project Zero at Harvard University in the 1990s (Perkins et al., 1993), also described a learning disposition via a triangular format that describes a combination of (a) inclination, (b) sensitivity to occasion, and (c) ability. These have been labelled as being *ready* (the inclination), *willing* (the sensitivity to the occasion) and *able* (the abilities and the experience or knowledge of the children and the teachers). It is the "sensitivity to occasion" that takes a disposition and capacity into a sociocultural frame and links to children being empowered to have an opinion. It insists that the "occasion" includes (in addition to the taonga) the opportunities, encouragements and invitations in the educational (and museum) environment that are central to the opportunities for children's creative capacities. In our discussions so far, this means central to *"growing raukura"* and central to *"creative capacity building"*:

> *E rite ana* [being ready]. Teachers, children and treasured objects will construct an environment in which curiosity is supported. Portfolios and paki ako provide local definitions of creative capacity and remind tamariki of those places where creativity is culturally and/or socially appropriate.

> *E whakaae ana* [being willing] and *e āhei ana* [being able]. Learners are empowered to contribute their own opinions and to do their own problem finding and problem-solving.

When teachers themselves model these aspects of an enduring attitude, they encourage children to feel safe enough to express uncertainty too, and for this uncertainty to translate into curiosity. For instance, examples of teachers sometimes being uncertain, and admitting to uncertainty, were eloquently employed in a research project described in Jerome Bruner's book *Actual Minds, Possible Worlds* (1986, p. 126). Carol Feldman was the researcher. She became interested in the situations when teachers indicated a sense of the hypothetical or uncertain, nature of knowledge; and she wondered if this might become an invitation to the children to be willing to come up with their own ideas, not waiting for a teacher's right answer. She recorded teachers' talk to each other in the staff room, and then she recorded their talk to students—noting expressions that contained modals of uncertainty and probability (like *might, could,* and so on). The results? Examples of expressing a stance of uncertainty or doubt in teacher talk to other teachers "far outnumbered their occurrence in teacher talk to students". The conclusion (in Bruner's words):

> The world that the teachers were presenting to their students was a far more settled, far less hypothetical, far less negotiatory world than the one they were offering to their colleagues (1986, p. 126).

In the language example in Chapter 1, for instance, Leanne was willing to admit that she "didn't know" the word in te reo, opening up a possible problem to be solved. She was also ready to recognise that this was a learning opportunity (the strengthening of the children's language expertise, te reo Māori, was never far from her mind); furthermore, she was both inclined and able to pursue this knowledge question—checking the dictionary for the right answer—and adding it as new knowledge in a *paki ako* [learning story; an assessment in narrative format for all the tamariki and ngā whānau. In the dramatic play example, the kaiako was willing to insist that "not anything goes"; to introduce a creativity principle. Ted responded with a creative solution. This accompanies the Te Whāriki curriculum principle of *whakamana*—ceding the initiative to the learner to find a problem and then to try to solve it—and is relevant to opportunities for children to be ready, willing and able to make their own creative contributions to museum visits (Figure 2.3).

Adding this example to all the children's portfolios (the tradition at Mana Tamariki) enacts the curriculum principle of whakamana (every child will experience an empowering curriculum that recognises and enhances the mana and supports them to enhance the mana of others). The message that this capacity is valued will be carried forward by this paki ako.

Cultural Anchor 3: *A te reol language as "the house of cultural sustainability"*

- Te tamaiti hei raukura (high achievers who exemplify the hopes and aspirations of their people) (Te Aho Matua, Ministry of Education, 2008, p. 746),
- a reifying of some of the stories and storying,
- te reo as "the house of cultural sustainability".

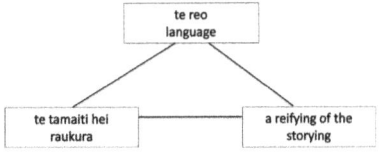

Figure 2.3 Cultural Anchor 3.

In order to describe their earlier research, the construction of a traditional garden at Mana Tamariki, Soutar et al. (2010, p. 36) drew a triangle: ngā paki ako, te tamaiti hei raukura, and ngā whānau with te reo at the centre. This was published in a chapter entitled *Growing Raukura*, by Soutar et al. (2010, p. 38), including whānau. In the Chapter 1 example from Mana Tamariki, it was noted that adding this example (of a paki ako [learning story]) to all the children's portfolios (the tradition at Mana Tamariki) enacts the curriculum principle of *whakamana* [every child will experience an empowering curriculum that recognises and enhances their mana and supports them to enhance the mana of others].

In a version of this triangle, for this chapter, we have emphasised te reo, supported by the storying in the children's portfolios and the ambition for the tamariki to become high achievers who exemplify the hopes and aspirations of their people. Brenda Soutar with Te Whānau o Mana Tamariki writes:

> During those foundation years [between 1990 to 1995] we actively sought the greater understanding of sociolinguistics. We embraced key international theories, in particular the work of Joshua Fishman (1991) and Bernard Spolsky (1998), both of whom confirmed the whānau development model as essential—in other words, children and families as active participants and leaders in the revitalisation of their language and culture.
>
> (Soutar et al., 2010 p. 36)

In 1995, Mana Tamariki introduced, for all new families, a policy that required at least one parent to commit to speak only te reo Māori to all the children enrolled in Mana Tamariki including their own. In recent years, the policy was strengthened to require both parents to make that commitment.

In education generally, children's communications—and adults' too—are frequently multi-modal: spoken words accompanied by gestures, exclamations and common-knowledge expressions. An earlier project in a different early childhood centre in Auckland, New Zealand's largest city (Carr et al., 2010) illustrated this modal complexity. In that centre, there were a number of four-year-olds for whom English was not their home language. We wrote the following in a description of an episode of play with a group of four-and-a-half year-olds who had, at home, been watching the same television programmes. Here is a comment from our description of one of the episodes.

> There is a sense in which Jack's play was 'multilingual'; he had added to his English, Mandarin and painting a shared community language, especially with Tom, that featured common characters and storylines and words (hotshot, power, transformers, missiles, 'cancelling the project', Optima and Cybertron) (p. 46).

Neil Mercer and Karen Littlejohn (2007), in their book entitled *Dialogue and the Development of Children's Thinking: A Sociocultural Approach*, remind us that:

> By harnessing the power of talk for reasoning and learning, children become more able to engage sociably and effectively with others, to benefit from reasoned dialogue with their teacher and peers, and ultimately to be empowered as earners with the reasoning capabilities necessary to rise creatively to the challenges posed by an uncertain future (p. 112).

Lesley Rameka and Brenda Soutar (2019, pp. 45–56) describe the recent stronger emphasis on the promotion of te reo Māori in all early years centres in Aotearoa New Zealand. As one example, they comment on the addition of whakataukī in the 2017 update of the Te Whāriki early childhood curriculum. Whakataukī can be viewed as "sayings, proverbs, prophecies, witticisms or mottos"; they are "able to provide ideas, concepts, and values in concise and often poetic ways that resonate with the heart" (p. 49). They are a link to the wise counsel of the ancestors providing clear messages for future generations (moko [grandchildren]), as illustrated by the following whakataukī from *Te Whariki* (Ministry of Education, 2017). They

Thinking in Triangles 27

strengthen the social ecosystem, making and cementing connections with the ancestral domain.

Tū mai e moko. Te whakaata o ō mātua. Te moko o ō tūpuna.
Stand strong, o moko. The reflection of your parents. The blueprint of your ancestors (p. 17).

An English language example of this notion of "anchors" as semiotic materials is Jay Lemke's (2000) discussion of "Artifacts, Activities, and Meanings in Ecosocial Systems". He writes of an object in a classroom (a student's notebook, for instance) that materially links events across time and space. As a material-semiotic object, it uses writing and drawing as a way of anchoring the pedagogy. In both our education sites, that anchoring is documented, over time, in portfolios of learning stories, often handwritten accounts, and sometimes dictated by the children (see Rose in Chapter 6); the two examples in Chapter 1 included learning stories of the events, written by the teachers and sent home to whānau. Their portfolios also provide a way of describing a "going-on" of the learning (see Chapter 8 in this book for more discussion on storying as an assessment mode at Mana Tamariki and Tai Tamariki) (Figure 2.4).

Cultural Anchor 4: Kaitiakitanga/Trusteeship

- Wisdom,
- an understanding and commitment towards a "common-good",
- *kaitiakitanga*/trusteeship.

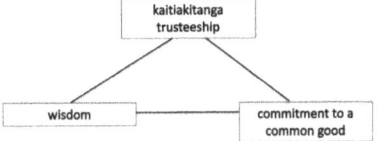

Figure 2.4 Cultural Anchor 4.

The discussion of creativity, wisdom and trusteeship going hand in hand in education has been eloquently made in the 2008 book entitled *Creativity, Wisdom and Trusteeship* edited by Anna Craft, Howard Gardner and Guy Claxton (2008), a book arguing that trusteeship is fundamentally about looking after culturally valued directions for creative capacity building. In effect, they develop a triangle that adds creativity and a "common-good" to "trusteeship": to look for those "good values" that a collaborative and creative triangle of builders (tamariki, kaiako and taonga) will hold in trust for present and future generations.

The authors were inspired by the finding, during the GoodWork Project from Harvard (see Fischman et al., 2004), that there was "a decreasing tendency among ambitious young people to prioritise the common good". Craft, Gardner and Claxton warned that:

> [C]reativity as played out in education and in work is vulnerable to a variety of forms of "blindness", including a disregard for diversity in culture and values, a lack of engagement with the question of how we might foster wisdom, increasing barriers to doing good work through decreasing trust, and a hesitation to assume responsibility for improving society.
>
> (Craft et al., 2008, p. 6)

We introduced Anna Craft in Chapter 1, adding warnings when she argued that:

> (T)he first blind spot is culture. I argue that policy calls for creativity in some universalized form are made without reference to or regards for macrocultural or subcultural values and approaches to life.... The discourse around creativity is one in which high value is placed on individuality.... The second blind spot relates to ethics and the environment, and it stems from the anchoring of creativity in the marketplace in this apparently culture-free way.
>
> (Craft et al., 2008, p. 19)

Collaborations between kaiako, tamariki and taonga during visits to museums (widely defined) can provide trustees and custodians for cultural values as well as for wise and creative educational outcomes. Guy Claxton (2008) emphasised the connection between wisdom and trusteeship "Wisdom takes account of the greater good and of one's higher, deeper and more lasting values" (p. 41). Furthermore, writing about "blind spots" in the creativity discourse.

We interpret trusteeship and kaitiakitanga as owing a debt to the past and to the ancestors, to the makers of the taonga and the things, and to the taonga and things themselves, for their role in humanity's life stories. Trusteeship and kaitiakitanga is a theme that will provide a subtext in each of the next four chapters of "coordinates" that assist and guide this creative capacity-building journey. Craft had insisted that narratives of the "common-good" set up worthwhile aspirations. Jerome Bruner adds the role of *trusteeship, kaitaiakitanga* to this Cultural Anchor, reminding us that narratives are "serious business".

One truth is surely self-evident: for all that narrative is one of our evident delights, it is serious business. For better or worse, it is our preferred, perhaps even our obligatory medium for expressing human aspirations and their vicissitudes, our own and those of others.... *It specialises in what is in jeopardy or what is presumed to be in jeopardy.*

(Bruner, 2002, pp. 89–90, our italics)

Those domains were introduced in Chapter 1 as three of five early childhood curriculum commitments. Te Whāriki introduced two more: mana reo (language) and mana aotūroa (exploration): an obligation to protect te reo, the Māori language, and (one of the outcomes in mana aotūroa) a capacity for "playing, imagining, inventing and experimenting" (Ministry of Education, 2017, p. 25).

In a volume of Māori writers writing about *Māori and the Environment: Kaitiaki* (Selby et al., 2010, p. 1) the editors write in an Introduction "Kaitiakitanga is an inherent obligation we have to our tupuna [ancestors] and to our mokopuna [grandchildren] to safeguard and care for the environment for future generations". Taonga and objects in museums are deemed to be valuable; visiting them can enable an understanding of their value and encourage the visitors to care about them and take on the messages about the ecology of the planet and the life and cultures within it.

It is a matter of identity, and perhaps, in both non-Māori and Māori discourse, we might use the words of Markus and Nurius (1986) to say that this caring can strengthen "possible selves": *possible selves* as kaitiaki or trustees for the protection of the taonga for future generations. It includes a link between the past and the future, the old and the new, between the taonga of the natural environment and tangata whenua (people of the land). It is part of the social ecology, creativity-building system.

> Kaitiakitanga is not an obligation which we choose to adopt or ignore; it is an inherited commitment that links mana atua, mana tangata and mana whenua, the spiritual realm with the human world and both of those with the earth and all that is on it.
>
> (Selby et al., 2010, p.1)

Coordinates for navigating the creative capacity building

These four anchors have provided us with a way of securing some places from which to interpret the museum visits as *cultural* journeys before we describe some of the creative capacity-building journeys themselves in the next four chapters. Interactions in the museums and the landscapes, and back at the early childhood centres, shone a light into ways to describe creative capacity-building encounters. Those encounters highlighted four interpretive coordinates. In those chapters, we continue the metaphor about travel, to describe them under the rubric of four "coordinates". We were gifted the title "he taonga, he rerenga arorangi" by the Mana Tamariki authors: "where there are treasured objects the spirit will be nurtured and creativity will be inspired". Unpacking this title, with young children, museum visits and creative capacity building in mind is the task for Chapter 7. In Chapter 8, we consider the "going-on" of "creative capacity building", and we ask: "What, exactly, is going on?"

Chapters 3–6 describe and provide examples of those four coordinates that provided directions for the creative capacity building: the children were gathering information, developing relationships, imagining, and using a range of modes to express their experiences and viewpoints, to story and restory. The two contexts enable the cultural anchors to underpin the weaving and unravelling of competing cultural storylines, and each chapter concludes with a commentary on the opportunities for the long-term goals of kaitiakitanga and trusteeship. The chapters are as follows:

Chapter 3: *E Rangahau Ana—Gathering Information.* Learning/knowing part of the stories of taonga/objects. Kaiako and tamariki become knowledgeable about the taonga and objects, and their past history.

Chapter 4: *E Whakawhanaunga Ana—Growing Relationships.* Restorying and restoring taonga/objects to life. Time is spent with the taonga, allowing them to "speak" their stories and the kaiako and tamariki to come to care about them.

Chapter 5: *E Waihanga Ana—Imagining Possibilities.* Imagination is wrapped around information about the taonga/objects.

Chapter 6: *E Whakaahua Ana—Multiplying Modes.* Representing perceptions and encouraging further stories.

The last two chapters build from the discussions in this chapter and Chapter 1, and the four coordinates to raise further topics for a conversation about creative capacity building and the dialogue across differences.

Chapter 7: Exploring the combinatory nature of the four coordinates (how they reach out to each other).

Chapter 8: The ongoing nature of the four coordinates (how they might be described as a creative capacity building that is *going on*). This discussion also returns us to the theme of creative capacity builders as kaitiaki and trustees.

Note

1 Children as Raukura: "'kia tu hei raukura mo tona iwi' are high achievers who exemplify the hopes and aspirations of their people" (Mataira, 1987).

References

Biesta, G. J. J. (2013). *The beautiful risk of education*. Paradigm.
Bruner, J. (1986). *Actual minds, possible worlds*. Harvard University Press.
Bruner, J. (1990). *Acts of meaning*. Harvard University Press.
Bruner, J. (2002). *Making stories: Law, literature, life*. Harvard University Press.
Carr, M., Smith, A. B., Duncan, J., Jones, C., Lee, W., & Marshall, K. (2010). *Learning in the making: Disposition and design in early education*. Sense.
Claxton, G. (2008). Wisdom: Advanced creativity? Chapter 3 In A. Craft, H. Gardner & G. Claxton (Eds.), *Creativity, wisdom and trusteeship* (pp. 35–48). Corwin.
Craft, A., Gardner, H., & Claxton, G. (2008). *Creativity, wisdom and trusteeship*. Corwin.
Dewey, J. (1938). *Experience and education*. The Macmillan Company.
Fischman, W., Solomon, B., Greenspan, D., & Gardner, H. (2004). *Making good: How young people cope with moral dilemmas at work*. Harvard Univerity Press.
Hutchins, E. (2005). Material anchors for conceptual blends. *Journal of Pragmatics, 37*, 1555–1577. http://www.cogsci.ucsd.edu/~faucon/BEIJING/hutchins.pdf
Ingold, T. (2012). Towards an ecology of materials. *Annual Review of Anthropology, 41*, 427–442. 10.1146/annurev-anthro-081309-145920
Lemke, J. (2000). Across the scales of time: Artifacts, activities, and meanings in ecosocial sytems. *Mind, Culture, and Activity, 7*(4), 273–290. 10.1207/S15327884MCA0704_03
Markus, H., & Nurius, P. (1986). Possible selves. *American Psychologist, 4*(9), 954–969. 10.1037/0003-066X.41.9.954
Mataira, K. (1987, 29 September). *Te Aho Matua o ngā Kura Kaupapa Maori: An interpretation of the Māori language document*. Part of a submission to the Associate Minister of Education by Te Runanga Nui o ngā Kura Kapapa Māori.
Matamua, R. (2017). *Matariki: The star of the year*. Huia.
Mercer, N., & Littleton, K. (2007). *Dialogue and the development of children's thinking: A sociocultural approach*. Routledge.
Ministry of Education. (2008). *Te Aho Matua o ngā kura kaupapa Māori and an explanation in English*. file:///Users/mdrum/Downloads/Supplement_TeAho32Feb08%20(3).pdf
Ministry of Education. (2017). *Te Whariki*. https://www.education.govt.nz/assets/Documents/Early-Childhood/Te-Whariki-Early-Childhood-Curriculum-ENG-Web.pdf

Ministry of Research, Science and Technology. (2005). *Vision mātauranga: Unlocking the innovation potential of Māori knowledge, resources and people.* https://www.mbie.govt.nz/assets/9916d28d7b/vision-matauranga-booklet.pdf

Perkins, D., Jay, E., & Tishman, S. (1993). Beyond abilities: A dispositional theory of thinking. *Merrill-Palmer Quarterly, 39*(1), 1–21.

Rameka, L., & Soutar, B. (2019). Te hōhonutanga o te Whāriki: Developing a deeper understanding of te Whāriki. In A. Gunn & J. Nuttall (Eds.), *Weaving te whāriki: Aotearoa New Zealand's early childhood curriculum document in theory and practice* (3rd ed., pp. 45–56). NZCER.

Selby, R., Moore, P., & Mulholland, M. (Eds.). (2010). *Māori and the environment: Kaitiaki.* Huia.

Soutar, B., with Te Whānau o Mana Tamariki. (2010). Growing raukura. In A. Meade (Ed.), *Dispersing the waves: Innovation in early childhood education* (pp. 35–40). NZCER.

3 E Rangahau Ana: Gathering Information

Intelligence cannot develop without matter to think about ... The more ideas about something people already have at their disposal, the more new ideas occur.... Knowing enough about things is one prerequisite for wonderful ideas.
(Eleanor Duckworth, 1987, p. 14)

The kōwhiti whakapae pattern, a weaving depicted in the ECE curriculum for Aotearoa New Zealand, symbolises the start of a journey that will take the traveller beyond the horizon.
(New Zealand Ministry of Education, 2017, p. 11)

Gathering information [E rangahau ana] is the first of the coordinates to guide creative capacity building in the early years. During visits to museums and places where taonga are found, we became very interested in what the children noticed and appeared to be gathering information about. How—and what—were the children apparently coming to know enough to create their own versions of the museums' storying? Diverse and diverting exhibits and places where treasured objects are found illustrated some answers. For the tamariki (children) at the Mana Tamariki kōhanga and kura, this included the *pou* (a carved post at Te Manawa, their local museum, representing the journey of Okatia, a spirit being), an indigenous kite (also at the local museum), and the landscape around the local Manawatu River. For the children at Tai Tamariki kindergarten, this included various exhibits in an exhibition entitled *Tyrannosaurs: Meet the Family* at Te Papa Tongarewa, their nearby museum. There were a number of "authors" during this meaning-making: children, taonga[1] (in an exhibition or landscape) and kaiako (teachers, including at Tai Tamariki the accompanying university visitors, also qualified early childhood teachers, who had permission to frequently take on a collaborative and

DOI: 10.4324/9781003313601-3

enquiring role), potentially providing opportunities for the children to gather enough information to inspire "wonderful ideas", as Eleanor Duckworth had suggested, or to do "some astonishing thinking" as Edwin Hutchins, in Chapter 2 of this book, might have predicted. It is the process of gathering that information that we explore in this chapter.

E rangahau ana—Information gathering at Mana Tamariki

Mana Tamariki's exhibition journey with Te Manawa Ahakoa Museum, within walking distance from te kōhanga ki te kura, gave the kaiako the opportunity to explore the stories of Okatia, a spirit being, and the Manawatu River. The first exhibit, creating a lot of talk and interest by the children at Mana Tamariki was their visit, with two kaiako, to the pou, carved in the 1980s and representing the story of the (local) Manawatu river and landscape formed by Okatia, a spirit being. An accompanying kaiako wrote up that visit for the tamariki and their whānau:

> On our first trip to Te Manawa we met Okatia, the carved pole. Brenda explained the story of Okatia. That's when we heard of the mana of Okatia in this district. Brenda explained that Okatia was a supernatural spiritual being that lived in a Tōtara tree. Okatia created the Manawatū Gorge and the river. You all listened intently, amazed perhaps by the height of the huge pole? Taller than you all, taller than Brenda. It almost reached the ceiling didn't it even though the ceiling itself is very high. As I looked up my neck hurt it was so tall. Was it the same for you?
>
> Some of you moved to get a better view. Some studied the carved parts, moving right around the pole as you looked. You were exploring, caressing, touching the carving. Some stood right back and observed the artwork.
>
> There was much conversation about the carvings (of birds and animals). Perhaps the bright colours and contemporary symbols made it easier for you all to understand the story being told. Exploring was exciting and identifying the different animals became a game. The stories of the pou were told through your excitement, "It's an eel, look an eel", "That's a tree!", "A river", "The Manawatū river", "A bird, a bird, Whaea!".

Then you debated which bird. Some said it was a huia. Perhaps because of our work studying Te Rau Huia, the formal entranceway at Mana Tamariki. Kātahi ka taukumekumetia te momo manu (Then the type of bird was debated). Te A., I think it was you who corrected us and told us it could not be a huia because the huia was a black bird, "No, that bird is blue, the huia was black". Someone else said it was a tūī. I thought it might be a kōkako becasue of it's blue colouring. M. said, "It's a native pigeon." Because of its large size most of us agreed.

We hadn't yet looked at any other areas in Te Manawa Ahakoa (the museum) but I could tell by the deep conversation about Okatia, we would be back.

Following the exhibition, the children began to think about the retelling of stories and how essential knowledge was passed down through *oriori*. These are traditional tribal chants composed for children, usually by their grandparents or elders. The chants are long, complex and talk of significant stories, features of landscape and relationships with people and place. The chants were composed before a child was born or at birth and sung repeatedly so the child acquired the words and tune and could recall the information in adulthood as needed. In this way, the chants were a spiritual awakening rather than a song to put the child to sleep. The child was being nurtured to be alert to the aspirations of her/his ancestors and the legacies and responsibilities to be carried forward in her/his time. The purpose of the oriori is to equip the child with the required knowledge to fulfil their role as a leader. In addition to kaiako (teachers) at kōhanga reo and kura, and whānau (family) at home, museums are one of several community places where space is made outside of te ao Māori (the Māori world) for people to engage with te ao Māori; they are places where the community can honour the past and engage children with their ancestors' legacy to assist their resiliency as Māori. In this chapter, we include an encounter as an example of *rangahau*, a translation of information gathering aligned to kaupapa Māori—Māori philosophy—which "... gives voice to Māori aspirations and expresses the ways in which aspirations, ideas and learning practices can be framed and organised" (New Zealand Ministry of Education, 2017, p. 61).

Rangimatua, an art exhibit in progress at the local museum

During another visit to the local museum, Rakei Te Kura shows his interest in an exhibition that was being set up by the artist.

36 E Rangahau Ana: Gathering Information

Rangimatua is a contemporary art piece, a large box structure. Rakei Te Kura is amazed and curious about the stylish hip-hop representation of a tupuna that exhibits both the old and new worlds. As the artist assembles the pieces together Rakei Te Kura draws the artwork in his sketchbook. The kaiako asks him some questions about what has captured his attention and why; she is encouraging him to take the time with his observing and drawing to develop an understanding and an intuitive sensation or feeling.

Speaker	Te reo Māori	English translation
Kaiako:	He aha ki a koe ngā painga o tēnei toi?	What is it that you like about this artwork? What to you is the benefit of this art?
Rakei Te Kura:	Ko tōku tino ko te pōtae, ā, a muri ka tā i ngā karu, me te ngutu, me te waha, me te arero.	I like the hat, the hat is my favourite, and then I'm going to draw the eyes. Then the lips, the mouth and the tongue.
Kaiako:	He pai ki a koe? He aha ai?	Do you like it? Why? Do you "like" it ... like = a total feeling encompassing spiritual response, physical, intuitive, how it makes you feel
Rakei Te Kura:	Āe, nā te mea he mahi toi.	Yes, because it is art.
Kaiako:	He aha te rerekētanga o tēnei momo toi ki ērā whakairo?	What is the difference between this art and the traditional carvings over there?
Rakei Te Kura:	He rākau ērā, ā, he tawhito.	They are wood and they are ancient. (He tawhito in this context means "ancient and connected to the spiritual realm where the spirits dwell, those who have gone before us").
Kaiako:	Me tēnei?	And this one?
Rakei Te Kura:	He tae me te moko ngā hū	This one has colour and a moko [tattoo] and shoes
Kaiako	He pātai āu mō te kaitoi? Tērā pea he mea kāore koe i te mōhio, i te mārama rānei? Kei te āhua whakamā a Rakei Te Kura.	Do you have any questions for the artist? Is there anything that you want to know about maybe? Rakei Te Kura is shy and quiet.

(Continued)

E Rangahau Ana: Gathering Information 37

Speaker	Te reo Māori	English translation
Artist	Kua kitea kē i tētahi mea pēnei i mua? Ki tētahi atu wāhi? Ki te pouaka whakaata?	Have you seen something like this before? Somewhere else? Maybe on TV?
Rakei Te Kura	Ki te pouaka whakaata	On TV

There is a shift in the conversation here. The kaiako cues Rakei te Kura into leading a conversation with the artist—to be courageous, express curiosity and gather information about the meaning and the background of the artwork. She "translates" but does not take over, and the artist follows her lead by speaking directly to the student in reply. We might describe this as whakamana/empowerment (see the Cultural Anchors in Chapter 2) in the making. Rakei te Kura then is bold enough to ask two questions about details in the artwork that he is curious about: the shoes, and the "things on his tongue". These turn out to be good aspects to be curious about; the latter was especially relevant to the creative purpose of the artwork.

Kaiako:	He aha ō pātai? Tukuna. Kei te pai.	What questions do you have? Ask them. It's OK.
Rakei Te Kura:	Te pōtae	The hat.
Kaiako:	Kei te hiahia koe ki te pātai he aha e mau hū nei tēnei hanga?	Do you want to ask why the exhibit is wearing a hat and shoes?
Rakei Te Kura:	Āe	Yes
Kaiako: (to Rakei Te Kura)	Pātai atu. Kia kaha.	Ask him. Be courageous
Kaiako (to the the artist)	Kei te hiahia ia ki te mōhio ki te take kei te mau hū, kei te mau pōtae.	He would like to know why this person is wearing a hat and shoes.
Artist (to Rakei Te Kura)	Kei te mau hū, kei te mau pōtae te tangata nei i te mea e hāngai ana ki te here i te ao o inanahi ki te ao o naianei. Ko te whakaatu i te tapu o te māhunga me te kawe mai i ngā whakaaro a ngā	He is wearing a hat and shoes because ... it is about showing connection from the ancient times and the now. The sacredness of the head, and the head holding the knowledge of

(*Continued*)

Kaiako:	He aha ō pātai? Tukuna. Kei te pai.	What questions do you have? Ask them. It's OK.
	mātua tīpuna, me te whakaaro he pēhea e mau i ō rātou korero mai i ngā wā o ngā rangatira mau huruhuru manu pēra ki te Huia, te mau atu i ērā momo ki ngā kākahu hou. Ko ētahi o ngā kaiwhakairo o roto o Te Arawa i timata rātou ki te whakairo i ngā hū kaupoi, engari kāore i tino whakaaengia e ngā tohunga whakairo engari i mahi tonu rātou. He whakaatu i te whakaaro auaha.	our ancestors, and I was thinking about how to hold on to their stories from the times when the chiefs were adorned with bird feathers, like the Huia and to wear these ancient treasures with the new clothes of today. Some carvers from Te Arawa began carving cowboy boots on their carvings. However, the master carvers were not so accepting of it, but they continued doing it. It showed their creative thinking.
Rakei Te Kura (to the artist)	Me ngā hū?	And the shoes?
Artist (in reply)	He orite te whakaaro o te here i te ao o mua ki te ao o naianei, e hikoi ana i te ao tawhito ki te ao hou nei i roto i ēnei hū hou. E hāngai ana ki te whakawhitinga ki te ao hou.	It's a similar concept of the bringing the old into the new, like walking from the old world into this new world in these new shoes. It's about the journey into the new world.
Kaiako	He roa ki te hanga?	Did it take you long to create?
Artist	Kōtahi tau au e rangahau ana e whakaaro ana me te ono marama ki te hanga.	I spent about a year researching and gathering information and about six months of that year I was creating the exhibit
Rakei Te Kura	He aha ērā mea ki tōna ārero?	What are those things on his tongue?
Artist	Ko ērā ngā whatu i kitea e Tāne i te Wharekura i te wā i piki ake ia i ngā rangi ki te kimi i ngā kete o te wānanga. E ai kī ētahi iwi ka tukuna ngā whatu ki tō waha i te wā	Those are the initiation stones that Tāne found in the Wharekura when he climbed to the heavens in search of the baskets of knowledge. It is said in some tribes that the

(*Continued*)

Kaiako:	He aha ō pātai? Tukuna. Kei te pai.	What questions do you have? Ask them. It's OK.
	he wānanga tapu. Nā reira ko taku hiahia ko te whakaatu i ngā tikanga tapu me ngā mahi a ngā tīpuna.	stones were to be put in your mouth when in a sacred wānanga. So, I wanted to show the ancient rituals and processes that our ancestors used.

While at the museum Rakei Te Kura draws a picture of the head and the hat. It is a drawing of the exhibit. About three weeks later back at school the class were asked to draw a picture that depicts the story of the creation of the Manawatū River. Okatia (the spirit being introduced earlier, in chapter two, with reference to the carved pou in the museum), lived in a tōtara tree. Through a desire to travel to the sea, Okatia caused the tree to topple and begin a journey toward the sea. During the course of this adventure, Okatia carved a path through the mountains and created the Manawatū Gorge between two mountain ranges, Tararua and Ruahine. These are some of the significant geographical features of the local region (Figure 3.1).

Rakei Te Kura drew the attached picture of Rangimatua, the ancestor figure in the artwork in progress in the museum. He has added a surround: mountain ranges, the Manawatu river, and the pou, as well as creative flourishes in the drawing and in his explanation (the bird feathers in the artwork have become a bird; the shoes have become jandals[2]). He describes it to the kaiako, a reminder of his visit to the developing museum exhibit, which included a hat and shoes and a connection between the old and the new worlds.

> He is an ancestor who lived in a time before there were cities. There were only mountains, rivers and marae. He had a staff that he carried everywhere and his friend was a bird. The bird is his pet. He is wearing a hat and some jandals to show the new world even though he lives in the old world.

Creative capacity building and kaitiakitanga/trusteeship

The pedagogy here was a sensitive balance between occasionally making suggestions and occasionally handing the authority back to the child (tamaiti); it was thus an example of whakamana/empowerment (one of

40 *E Rangahau Ana: Gathering Information*

Figure 3.1 Rangimatua: Drawing by Rakei Te Kura.

the cultural anchors, in chapter two) at work. The notion that information-gathering for a creative construction is worthy of a lengthy period of research, from many sources, was eloquently described by the artist in the museum. What is being held in trust here? In Cultural Anchor 4, we argued that trusteeship is a looking forward: a holding something in trust, supported by wisdom and an understanding and commitment towards a "common good" vision. Furthermore, if, as we began to surmise, it is *creative capacity building*—linked to information—*that will be held in trust*, the artist modelled this, the kaiako encouraged it, and the five-year-old enhanced and enriched his "store" of creative capacity when he demonstrated (with kaiako encouragement) his curiosity, made his own drawing and told his own story.

Rakei Te Kura, as a member of the local iwi (tribe) to whom the stories of local place belong. His genealogical connection to the

Manawatū river, the mountain ranges and Okatia support his information gathering. Part of his role as a kaitiaki is also to maintain and protect the stories of his ancestors. For Māori, kaitiakitanga is connected to whakapapa (genealogy), and "Everything has a whakapapa: birds, fish, animals, trees, and every other living thing; soil, rocks and mountains also have a whakapapa" (Barlow, 1991, p. 173). Many of these features are included in Rakei te Kura's drawing. Here, he strengthens his own identity and sense of belonging within the contemporary world. His picture of Rangimatua drew upon his encounter with the artist at the museum and gives a creative context to his connections between the old and new worlds; the cultural narrative left room for original additions.

E rangahau ana—Information gathering at Tai Tamariki

Tai Tamariki Kindergarten was introduced in Chapter 1. We documented the children's visits to an exhibition at Te Papa Tongarewa (the New Zealand National Museum in the capital city, Wellington): *Tyrannosaurs—Meet the Family*, advertised for schools as "an immersive multimedia experience that explores how these tyrannical dinosaurs, with their massive skulls, powerful jaws, and bone-crunching teeth became the world's top predators". It included a tyrannosaur family tree, a model of a recently discovered feathery relative of T rex, life-size models of dinosaurs (many of them moving in realistic fashion) and an interactive exhibit which represented the destructive power of the meteor that killed the dinosaurs.

For the Tai Tamariki young children (aged three and four years), visits to Te Papa's exhibition included not just the models of dinosaurs, but also interactive exhibits, life-size dioramas of dinosaurs in boats, and movies of dinosaurs running along with the city of Wellington Harbour precinct, near the museum. In this chapter, we describe three-year-old Jack's mode of dramatically illustrating his gathering of information in one of the interactive exhibits.

Jack and the meteor

Three-year-old Jack, accompanied by Jeanette, a visiting university early childhood education teacher, approaches an interactive exhibition that illustrates a meteor crashing onto the Earth. The museum exhibit, plus Jeanette, provided the initial information about the demise of the dinosaurs. A platform represents the arrival of the meteor, and the visitor must jump vigorously on it to represent the meteor's travel to earth. When a button is pressed, prior to the jump, an arrow indicates the size of the on-coming meteor, representing the vigour of the visitor's jump. Jack has watched some school children interacting with this exhibit.

Jeanette: Tell me about what happens there (points to the meteor crash/jump site exhibit).
Jack: You jump! Jump on it, crash!
Jeanette: (Pointing to a green button on the exhibit) All right, so then can you see that little green, what that's, that arrow's telling you to do with that button?
Jack jumps.
Jeanette: [See that] button up there? See that?
Jack: Ready, set, go.
Jeanette: Press it, oh ok. ... . Oh-oh I see, we, no I still think we have to press the button ... (Jack presses the button) Yip. The harder you jump, [the bigger] the meteor you create.
(Jack jumps on the platform several times).
Jeanette: Ohhh! Look Jack, there you go! Look, watch it!
Jack jumps higher.
Jeanette: Oh, oh. You stamped out the dinosaurs Jack!
Jack: What?
Jeanette: You made a meteor ten kilometres wide.
Ok Jack, yeah, some other children are going to, want to have a go ...
Maybe just, maybe just come back out here. Come back in here Jack and maybe look. You're ... you did such a big crash ... you did such a big jump, that the meteor you created stamped out the dinosaurs!
So, you know how big that meteor is! Just, let's wait for some of these other groups to have a go.

Later, Jack returns to look at the diagram on the wall that illustrated the meteor crashing.

Jack: (Explaining to Jeanette, who has returned with him): This is the ones where the dinosaurs (pause) and here's some more dinosaurs on this *(gestures to a timeline on the wall).*
Jeanette: So, what's this telling us?
Jack: This telling us which dinosaurs lived in the day of the dinosaurs (waves his hand over the timeline chart).
Jeanette: (Nods): In the different times.

Jack:	Yes, and there, because, um ...
Jeanette:	Oh, and some of them, it says up here ... .
Jack:	They all died from the big Meteora (he links his hands over his head)
Jeanette:	They all died from the big meteor?
Jack:	... clash into the water.

(He crouches down on the floor, saying in a sombre voice): And then they all died and here was, there was, the sky was all black, nothing there to grow. Then they all flopped down to the ground, and couldn't move (he flops his body sideways onto the floor, looking serious and sad).

Creative capacity building and trusteeship

Jack was eloquent, adding his own imaginative description to the information given: "they all died and there was, there was, the sky was all black, nothing there to grow". In this example, while it was the exhibit that outlined an initial storying, it was Jack who animated it by acting it out, restorying it to accompany his actions and his comment: "they all died and there was, there was, the sky was black, nothing there to grow". In this example, Jack wanted to return to this exhibit to look again at the diagram. This was an example of a three-year-old who was enabled to follow up on his curiosity and information gathering, returning to remind himself about what was interesting; in this case, the second viewing encouraged Jack's enactment and a description of the meteor story in his own words, creatively expanding the exhibit's initial story.

We look back to the final triangle in Chapter 2 to ask: What aims and outcomes were the teachers and the artefacts (together with the museum environments) holding "in trust" for the children? In this example, the demise of the dinosaurs was "felt", animated, via an interactive drama, as Jack, who was already very interested in dinosaurs, was enabled by the museum exhibit and the accompanying adult to dramatically and physically mimic the event and describe it, with an attitude of sadness. The topic of this exhibition provided an implicit custodial perspective: events can put animals at risk. To extrapolate a little, a sub-text of this exhibit (and this exhibition) was an implicit warning: in the 21st century we should remember the stories of the dinosaurs, and, by extension, care for animals and plants at risk of extinction—for example, from global warming. In the background, for Jack, was a sadness as well as the creative storying of these amazing animals from long ago.

Notes

1 "Objects", Tim Ingold argues, become "things" when they are "entangled in a skein of movement and affect" in the "web of life ecology" (2012, p. 437). DeLeuze and Guattari (1994, p. 164) comment as follows: "What is preserved—the thing or the work of art—is a *bloc of sensations, that is to say, a compound of percepts and affects*". Columbia University Press. This is certainly true about Okatia (in the landscape) for Mana Tamariki, and also the dinosaurs in the exhibition at Te Papa Tongawera National Museum. DeLeuze and Guattari (1994) What is Philosophy? London & New York: Verso.
2 Jandals are a type of sandal, usually made of rubber, with V-shaped support between the big toe and the other toes to support the foot.

References

Barlow, C. (1991). *Tikanga whakaaro*. Oxford University Press.
DeLeuze, G., & Guattari, F. (1994). *What is philosophy?* Verso.
Duckworth, E. (1987). *"The having of wonderful ideas" and other essays on teaching and learning*. Teachers College, Columbia University: Teachers College Press.
Ingold, T. (2012). Towards an ecology of materials. *Annual Review of Anthropology, 41*, 427–442. 10.1146/annurev-anthro-081309-145920
New Zealand Ministry of Education. (2017). *Te Whāriki: Early childhood curriculum*.

4 E Whakawhanaunga Ana: Growing a Relationship

Let me take, as one example, the whāriki that my great grandmother made. It is kept at Ngatokowaru, the marae that she helped to establish. It is cared for by one of my aunties, who learned from my Nanny the protocols for its storage and use. Being able to touch and handle something that our great grandmother made is naturally very special for her descendants. (Mikaere, 2006, p. 38)	Never in control of the situation, not knowing what any day will bring, the anthropological participant is vulnerable, largely at the mercy of unfolding events, and ever reliant on improvisation. ... Indeed, anthropological observation differs only in degree of intensity from what all people do all the time. (Ingold, 2018, p. 60)

Ani Mikaere provides an example of a relationship over time with taonga, in this case, a whāriki (weaving) that crosses the generations; the relationship included knowing the protocols for its preservation, and, in this case, the value of being able to touch and handle it.

In this chapter, we reflect on events and comments that describe children's relationships with taonga, or things,[1] in their local museum. One of the educational principles in Te Whāriki, the national bicultural and bilingual early childhood curriculum in Aotearoa New Zealand, introduced in Chapter 1, is *Relationships/Ngā hononga*. The curriculum states, as follows:

> It is through responsive and reciprocal relationships with people, places and things that children have opportunities to try out

DOI: 10.4324/9781003313601-4

their ideas and refine their working theories. For this reason, collaborative aspirations, ventures and achievements are valued.

Connections to past, present and future are integral to a Māori perspective of relationships. This includes relationships to tīpuna who have passed on and connections through whakapapa to, for example, maunga, awa, moana, whenua and marae[2].

(Ministry of Education, 2017, p. 21)

E whakawhanaungatanga—Growing a relationship at Mana Tamariki

Relationship building is included in the ways of approaching and engaging with an exhibition. Brenda describes as follows the protocols associated with a visit by a group of tamariki to an art gallery exhibition of artworks/taonga inspired by Tāne, the Māori god of the forest. They were travelling in a van to Wellington, another city in Aotearoa New Zealand. While thinking about the protocols for the children's visit, she emphasised that this engagement is central to the relationship building even before the tamariki and kaiako enter the art gallery's exhibition.

> One of the things we think is important is when we're documenting the process of engaging with the taonga, that we document the special way in which we approach and engage. So, Mana Tamariki, when they visited that exhibition of artwork entitled *Ko Tāne-pupuke* we got on the van and Michael sent us off with a karakia (blessing) and we chose Michael because he connects with this whenua (region). At the exhibition we had a mihi (greeting), we had a karakia, we went around, we talked to each Tāne (in this case, the art-works) and then the children got the sketch books and chose a place that they wanted to sit.

The calling of taonga engages relationships with earlier generations and with ancestors. It involves an "energy flow". Professor and kaumatua (esteemed Māori elder) Mason Durie outlines three reasons for introducing the spiral of ecological synergy into the discussion of indigenous views of the world. The first includes the concept of tūrangawaewae: "a term linking individuals with a site or location that underpins their identity, as well as their relatives"

E Whakawhanaunga Ana: Growing a Relationship 47

(2010, pp. 242-243). Second, "Just as people take on qualities derived from the natural environment, inanimate material objects possess their own form of life: a mauri, which both distinguishes them (from other objects) and also unites them within a wider network of entities". Third, "the spiral of ecological synergy is built around the dimension of time" (Durie, 2010, p. 243).

> Relationships in time are as important as spatial relationships and the ecological perspective, which underlines indigenous world views, places emphasis on both past and future relationships. The spiral (of ecological synergy) gains momentum from a distant past and travels out to a future, well beyond human comprehension.
>
> (Durie, 2010, pp. 243-244)

The kōhanga and kura regularly return to the local museum, following the same routine in which kaiako (teachers) offer tamariki (children) time to select a taonga to spend time with, and maybe to sketch. On each occasion, over four to five months, Taumaihiroa revisited and drew the same *manu aute* (traditional kite). Here are some of her drawings, and her conversation with the filmmaker (kaitukuata) as they looked together at her sketchbook. She dramatically illustrates the flying, restoring her ongoing relationship with the kite at each visit, and restorying as she draws, describes and animates by demonstrating: "Like this ... the wings go like this. She flies away. Then her legs fly. Then no flapping. ... (She) flies to the clouds where she hides". In one drawing she accompanies the kite with Tawhirimātea, the energy force or god of winds (Figures 4.1–4.4).

Speaker	Te reo Māori	English translation
Taumaihiroa	Ka taea e au te tuhi te manu aute?	Can I draw the kite?
Kaitukuata	Āe, haere mai ki te tiki i tō pukapuka.	Yes. Come and get your book.
Taumaihiroa	I te kōhanga au i tuhi au mō te manu aute	When I was in the kōhanga I sketched the kite.
Kaitukuata	He pai tonu ki a koe te manu aute?	Do you still like the kite?
Taumaihiroa	Āe, he, kei te rere. Kei te rere ia ki te katoa o ngā wāhi. Kātahi ka, ka taea ia te rere	Yes, it's flying. She's flying to all the places. And then, then she can fly.

Figure 4.1 Taumaihiroa's manu aute 1.

Figure 4.2 Taumaihiroa's manu aute 2.   Figure 4.3 Taumaihiroa's manu aute 3.

Taumaihiroa: jumping about, waving her arms	Ka pēnei na ... ka pēnei ngā parirau ka rere. Ka rere atu ia. Kātahi ka rere ōna waewae. Kātahi ka ... katahi kāore i te pakipaki. Ka rere noa pēnei.	Like this ... the wings go like this. She flies away. Then her legs fly. Then no flapping. Just flies like this.
Kaitukuata	Ka rere ki whea?	Flies where?
Taumaihiroa	Ka rere ki ngā kapua ka huna ia. Kātahi ka rere ōna parirau, kātahi ka rere atu ka rere ōna waewae.	Flies to the clouds where she hides. Then her wings fly and her legs fly.
Kaitukuata	Nā reira ka rere ia ki te ātea?	So, she flies into outer space?
Taumaihiroa	Kao, ka rere ia ... ka rere ia ki te rangi.	No, she flies ... she flies to the sky.

(*Continued*)

E Whakawhanaunga Ana: Growing a Relationship 49

Kaitukuata Taumaihiroa (jumping about):	Nē? E, ka peke ia ki te rangi, ka rere ōna waewae k ... kātahi ka huna ki ngā kapua.	Really? Yes, she jumps to the sky, her legs fly ... then hides in the clouds.
Kaitukuata	He pai ki a koe te manu aute?	Do you like the kite? [Do you "like" ... "like" = a total feeling encompassing a spiritual response, physical, intuitive, how it makes you feel].
Taumaihiroa	He manu aute tēnei. Ko tēnei he kōtiro manu aute, ā, ka rere pēnei na.	This is a bird kite. She is a girl kite and she flies like this.

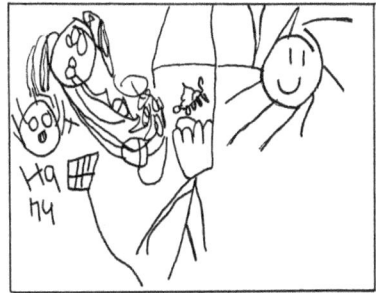

Figure 4.4 Taumaihiroa's manu aute & tāwhirimātea & tamanuiterā.

The final sketch drawn at the museum by Taumaihiroa is her revisiting a memory of flying her kite with her father. In conversations between the kaiako and parents, it is revealed that Tauimaihiroa often speaks to her parents about kites. Her parents purchase a kite. She draws Tāwhirimātea (the energy force/god of wind) and explains to her kaiako that the koru pattern is a representation of the wind and Tamanuiterā (the sun) is shining. The inclusion of Tamanuiterā and Tāwhirimātea in her drawing transforms her kite into a Māori kite.

Taumaihiroa	He Māori a Tāwhirimātea, ko ia te atua o te hau.	Tāwhirimātea is Māori, he is the atua of the winds. *atua* is an energy force in the natural environment. Together energy forces make up the natural world that humankind exists within. An energy force is present in the essence of the

(Continued)

Kaiako	Āe, kei te tika	domain they preside over, e.g., Tangaroa is the essence of everything in the domain of the sea. Yes, that's right
Taumaihiroa	Ā, he wera a Tamanuiterā, ā, he Māori rāua.	And Tamanuiterā is hot and, they are Māori.
Kaiako	Āe rā.	Yes, they are.
Taumaihiroa	Ko taku manu aute mai i te toa he Māori, he koru o Tāwhirimātea. He kōtiro ia, ā, ka rere, ka rere ki runga i te rangi ki ngā kapua	My kite from the shop is Māori, with koru (spiral pattern) of Tāwhirimātea. She is a girl and she flies, flies high in the sky to the clouds
Kaiako	Kei te hiahia koe kia manuaute koe ā tōna wā?	Do you want to be a kite when you grow up?
Taumaihiroa	Āe, āe ka hiahia au.	Yes, yes, I do.

E whakawhanaunga ana, growing a relationship, creative capacity building and kaitiakitanga

For Māori, whakapapa (genealogy) is the foundation of all relationships. Whakapapa defines how people relate and are related to each other and the natural environment. "Whakapapa connects us to everything there is, creating a myriad of relationships that speak to us of reciprocity, of responsibility and of the need for respect." Ani Mikaere, (2006, p. 33). In her role as a kaitiaki (trustee), Taumaihiroa continues a respectful and responsive relationship as she adds more ideas each time, personifying the kite in drawing and acting. There were enough adults accompanying the children to enable her to construct an extended encounter between the *taonga* (treasured objects), the *adult* (the filmmaker, who kept the conversation going), and *herself*—dancing, drawing and explaining—and the manu aute (kite) in the museum providing a *material anchoring* for Taumaihiroa's storytelling and re-telling ("she" "flies to the clouds where she hides") as well as her accompanying action.

E whakawhanaungatanga—Growing a relationship at Tai Tamariki

Changing the scale

In this example, Andrea, one of the teachers at Tai Tamariki takes the lead to choreograph a playful episode between children and materials.

E Whakawhanaunga Ana: Growing a Relationship 51

This was in response to some of the children talking about feeling afraid when they went on a visit to the exhibition *Tyrannosaurus Rex: Meet the Family*. She writes the following, including it in the two children's portfolios, and adds photographs taken during the play.

> Just before the holidays I hung a big (fabric) T Rex on the deck and let Bruce and Tom know there was a dinosaur on the deck! Look at you both, again being curious together and now asking more questions. "What is it doing here?" you asked. You two big guys quickly got closer and experimented with how it might move and Tom again used his knowledge of sounds to roar a convincing T Rex roar. See how much you both have grown and how you have learned many more ways of exploring and learning together.
>
> I just thought, when I get stuck for ideas, changing the scale's quite useful. When you've got big things, making them small. When you've got small things making it big or shadows. It seemed to be at the beginning a lot of their learning was around feeling scared because the dinosaur exhibition was so scary and so noisy. A lot of them were talking about feeling afraid and when I looked at it, it was definitely sound but also the huge projected images of dinosaurs stomping around the space they were in. They dwarfed us. I think that would have been quite fear-making.
>
> I had stitched little wind pockets on the feet as an experiment because I was hoping the dinosaur would flap about in the wind. It was an idea I had, but this day there was no wind so it hung there not moving! I was a little disappointed because it seemed that it didn't work. When you examined it Tom you instantly put your hands into the feet pockets and moved it like a dinosaur— Unexpectedly the dinosaur came to life before my eyes and I was amazed at how you made it so dinosaur like! It did work after all. Just not the way I thought it would. Bruce was also keen to play and this was a good experience for him because some of the dinosaurs upstairs were very scary for him. I think it was good for him to discover this with you and to play with scariness and courage. You might not have known it at the time but you and Bruce helped each other learn as well as have a great deal of fun. I laughed a lot that morning as did many other children that joined in as they said good bye to their Mums and Dads.

52 E Whakawhanaunga Ana: Growing a Relationship

Changing the story changes the relationship: Bruce not scared any more

This was a vivid example of the teacher constructing a creative storying with materials, and then the children altering the story, using the same material to change the relationship. Andrea's commentary indicates that her initiative, plus the *material* (the fabric dinosaur "shadow"), and the *children's engagement* meant that the dinosaur "came to life" in a way that was surprising but not "scary". She had assumed that the wind would make it move; however, with Tom initially taking the lead, the children became puppeteers, in charge of the movements that had been the problem for them in the actual exhibit. Her notion of "changing the scale" in this case shifted the agency; in a sense, she was also changing the *scale of the relationship* between the viewer and the viewed, in effect shifting the scale of the children's relationship with the enormous model dinosaurs in the museum.

Andrea: I've got lots of fabric that I had ready to go that we could have attached that could have really dangled and flapped and it could have really come alive and we could have made a jungle or we could have made red lava or all sorts. But because, I guess, because I wasn't rostered out there and then I was off I wasn't there to do it so I don't think they got hung up. But Bruce, I think the biggest thing I've seen with Bruce, he is so over it now, he's not scared anymore and I just saw this learning story that Maiangi (another teacher) made. It was really nice to read, he said that he would go up to the exhibition and take me and if I was scared, I could stand behind him.

Margaret: Oh, he said that to Maiangi?

Andrea: Yeah, and she put that in his story and he said he wanted it in his dinosaur profile book. He's really just clicked the whole profile book thing and if there's something he's interested in, he asks to put it in his profile book.

Margaret: So how old is Bruce?

Andrea: He's three. But that was really amazing because he just wouldn't go through the door the first time and his dad's got it on his phone, a clip of him looking just terrified climbing all over his mother saying "I want to go to kindergarten, I want to go to kindergarten" and then now, every day he still

E Whakawhanaunga Ana: Growing a Relationship

asks me if we can go up to—he calls it "my papa" and I think he called it the other papa, the other Te Papa and I said "do you mean the exhibition? Do you mean the big room where the dinosaurs were?" and now he's got this word for *exhibition*; his mum was telling it to me last night. I can't remember the word, it's a close version of it but it's cool because I don't think we took him up there too much but this exhibition's really been a turning point for him ....

Yeah. And now he just tears through there. Says he's not scared any more. I said "What happened to the scared?" and he said "I'm not scared anymore" ....

He's got great knowledge and has skills of making things and doing things, he's a real knowledge guy. ... I don't know if it's specifically because it's dinosaurs because you see he was so into trains before that; we really supported his trains and I think ... I think he's good at being interested in something. I've often thought: "Is it the dinosaurs or just that you've got a good process of learning or something?". I'm not sure how long this dinosaur interest will last. If we get another exhibition or another thing that comes in next year I'm wondering if he will still talk about the dinosaurs. There's activities he asks for, like he wants me to make more freezing of the ice and the dinosaurs and that would be nice to do at this end of it.

Note: Andrea had constructed an activity in which she froze small plastic dinosaurs in a block of ice and sand. Bruce and Tom were especially interested in this. They spent time digging the dinosaurs out, and one of the teachers assisted them to know the names.

Growing a relationship, creative capacity building and trusteeship at Tai Tamariki

We might describe these encounters with the fabric dinosaurs, the planning book, and the dinosaurs in the exhibition as "materially anchored blends" that include the children and the teachers. A material anchor, Edwin Hutchins says: "permits people to do some astonishing thinking" (see Hutchins, 2005, p. 1562, in Chapter 2). In this case, materially anchored blends—in Andrea's planning book and fabric construction, over time—were her tools for astonishing thinking. The teacher's material anchoring (the fabric dinosaurs) reduced the scale and enabled hands-on play by the children; it enhanced the learning and enabling the children to share the initiative for developing projects and interests over time.

All of the cultural anchors described in Chapter 2 of this book are at play in these improvised relationships: a space where the spirit (widely defined) is nurtured, an enabling of the children's voices, te reo (Māori language) as the "house of cultural sustainability", and visions of what is valued. In the title for one of the principles of the curriculum in both places, Te Whāriki, the pedagogy is about ngā hononga (relationships). In these examples, that pedagogy contributed to the way on which the relationships between the tamariki and the taonga/objects/things were unfolding, while still enabling the children to be in charge. In his book, Anthropology And/As Education, Tim Ingold (2018, p. 60) argues that "the purposes of anthropology, of the university, and of education itself are intimately bound up with one another". He adds, in what could be described as an eloquent description of these early childhood pedagogical practices:

> Typically, the participant observer will spend an extended period of many months or even years, joining in the lives of people in some place …. Never in control of the situation, not knowing what any day will bring, the anthropological participant observer is vulnerable, largely at the mercy of unfolding events, and ever reliant on improvisation. Her questions are never exhausted by their answers but always give way to further questioning, none of which comes any closer to a solution but which nevertheless opens up to an ongoing process of life.
>
> (Ingold, 2018, p. 60)

Notes

1 "Objects", Tim Ingold argues, become "things" when they are "entangled in a skein of movement and affect" in the "web of life ecology" (2012, p. 437). DeLeuze and Guattari (1994, p. 164) comment as follows: "What is preserved—the thing or the work of art—is a bloc of sensations, that is to say, a compound of percepts and affects". Columbia University Press. This is certainly true about Okatia (in the landscape) for Mana Tamariki, and also the dinosaurs in the exhibition at Te Papa Tongawera National Museum. DeLeuze and Guattari (1994). What is Philosophy? London & New York: Verso.
2 tīpuna, maunga, awa, moana, whenua and marae: ancestors, mountain, river, sea, ground and meeting area of whānau (extended family) or iwi (tribe).

References

DeLeuze, G., & Guattari, F. (1994). *What is philosophy?* Verso.
Durie, M. (2010). Outstanding universal value: How relevant is indigeneity? In R. Selby, P. Moore & M. Mulholland (Eds.), *Māori and the environment: Kaitiaki* (pp. 239–249). Huia.
Hutchins, E. (2005). Material anchors for conceptual blends. *Journal of Pragmatics, 37*, 1555–1577. http://www.cogsci.ucsd.edu/~faucon/BEIJING/hutchins.pdf
Ingold, T. (2018). *Anthropology and/as education*. Routledge.
Ingold, T. (2012). Towards an ecology of materials. *Annual Review of Anthropology, 41*, 427–442. 10.1146/annurev-anthro-081309-145920
Mikaere, A. (2006). Whakapapa and taonga: Connecting the memory. In E. Moore (Ed.), *Puna Maumahara: Rōpū Tuku Iho Repositories. Proceedings of a conference*. Te Wānanga o Raukawa.
Ministry of Education. (2017). *Te Whāriki: Early childhood curriculum*. https://www.education.govt.nz/assets/Documents/Early-Childhood/Te-Whariki-Early-Childhood-Curriculum-ENG-Web.pdf

5 E Waihanga Ana: Imagining

> Imagination is no mere ornament; nor is art. Together they can liberate us from our indurated habits. They might help us to restore decent purpose to our efforts and help us create the kind of schools our children deserve and our culture needs. Those aspirations, my friends, are stars worth stretching for.
> (Eisner, 2005, p. 214, The John Dewey Lecture of 2002)

> When the first European settlers arrived in Aotearoa in the late 1700s and early 1800s, they were astounded by the large amount of astronomical knowledge maintained by Māori. ... However, colonisation and its many attributes infiltrated to the core of Māori society, affecting all cultural practices, including Māori astronomy.
> (Matamua, 2017, p. 3)

Maxine Greene writes as follows in a paper ("Thinking of Things as if They Could be Otherwise") written for her students as part of an arts programme:

> I began last week with talk of imagination and the pursuit of identity. I was trying to call attention to the breakthroughs that occur, to the upsurges of the unexpected we may experience at certain moments of engagement with works of art. Most of us can summon up such moments. ... We experience a sense of surprise oftentimes, an acute sense that things might look otherwise, feel otherwise, *be* otherwise than we have assumed—and suddenly the world seems new, with possibilities still to be explored.
> (Greene, 2001, p. 116)[1]

As Maxine Greene has described it: "We are interested, you see, in enabling persons to multiply their perspectives, extend their visions, strive

DOI: 10.4324/9781003313601-5

E Waihanga Ana: Imagining 57

for new ways of apprehending the complex world" (2001, p. 49). We see this multiplying, extending and striving as central to the pursuit of *he taonga, he rerenga arorangi*: the freedom to soar to the heights of one's creative potential in a space where the spirit is nurtured, introduced as Cultural Anchor 1 in Chapter 2, and explored in Chapter 7.

In 1975, Jacob Getzels and Mihalyi Csikszentmihalyi wrote a chapter entitled From Problem Solving to Problem finding. They commented:

> How did we come to study the creativity of *problems* when we began by studying the creativity of *solutions*? How did we reach the conclusion that the creative act involves problem finding as much as it does problem solving (if the two processes can be separated at all), and to hold the hypothesis that creative problems may be as fruitful a subject of study as creative solutions?
>
> (1975, p. 90)

They noted that at that time of writing there was an abundance of studies on problem solving, but "virtually no systematic work on problem finding, the posing and formulating of problems" (Getzels & Csikszentmihalyi, 1975, p. 90). This coordinate, on imagining, is as much about problem finding as it is about problem solving; a support in Cultural Anchor 4: an understanding and commitment towards a "common good", a vision matauranga[2] (MoRST, 2007, p. 1), and very much influenced by the Māori title for our project, which talks about "unrestricted freedom to soar to the heights of one's creative potential in a space where the spirit is nurtured" (p. 22). Creativity is often associated with making unexpected connections—imaginative cognitive leaps. What we are proposing as distinctive is the idea that imaginative steps are more than cognitive and conceptual. To be robust they will be dispositional (reflecting ability, prior knowledge and inclination), situated (sensitive to the occasion), and exciting (entangled with effect). Our theorising of this coordinate was also supported by interviews with teachers in the kindergarten who explained their strategies for challenging the children to think "outside the box" (see, for instance, Andrea's comments in Chapter 4).

A forum and a temple

In his book *Voices of Collective Remembering*, James Wertsch (2002) makes a distinction between two museum perspectives. He proposes that exhibitions that take on a single committed perspective can be described as a "temple" where visitors come to learn about "reverently held stories", whereas those that encourage ambiguous interpretations present the museum as a "forum" (p. 42) and thus provide opportunities for discussion, dialogue, personal interpretation—and imagination (our addition). A museum exhibition as a forum presents multiple possible stories, and opportunities for visitors to embroider or enhance a museum storyline: to add to the information they have absorbed, to introduce their own creative responses and to provide opportunities for thoughtful problem finding, problem solving and dialogue. We will see some examples in this chapter. At Mana Tamariki, the children were finding and solving problems as they worked collaboratively on a project. At Tai Tamariki, Sarah was inventing—and then solving—perceived problems associated with the uncertain movements of very large dinosaur figures in the museum.

We have in mind the following comment from Debbie Meier (1995, 2002) the Principal and founder of the Central Park East School in East Harlem, writer of the books *The Power of Their Ideas* (1995) and *In Schools We Trust: Creating Communities of Learning in an Era of Testing and Standardisation* (2002). In the second of these two books she says:

> I like the fact that we are by nature unique, unpredictable, complex, never fully knowable, and endlessly varied. I'm glad that the real world doesn't come with built-in multiple-choice boxes, precoded and ready to score. ... The thing that keeps me going, on even the gloomiest days, is that element of potential surprise.
>
> (Meier, 2002, p. 181)

Surprise can begin a conversation about building creative capacities. We were often surprised, and so were the tamariki (children) and the kaiako (teachers). In the first Sarah example in this chapter, Maiangi, the teacher, introduced surprise into the conversation. In the second example, Sarah went to a great deal of work to create surprise: surprising both the teacher and, she thought, the dinosaur figure too.

Mihalyi Csiksentmihalyi (1990, p. 363) commented that "Creative people are constantly surprised. They don't assume that they understand what is happening around them, and they don't assume that anybody else does either". And Richard Sennett, in his book entitled *The Craftsman*, says "Surprise is a way of telling yourself that something you know can be other than you assumed" (2008, p. 211). Often, the catalyst for that surprise was an unsettling, uncertainty, that came from crossing the boundary from one community (the early childhood centre, for instance) to another (the museum, broadly defined, for instance). As Etienne Wenger (1998) has commented in his discussion of communities of practice: "as the boundaries of practice become part of our personal experience of identity, the work of reconciliation is an active, creative practice" (p. 161). In Chapter 2, for instance, we described a group of three-year-olds from Tai Tamariki, visiting an art exhibition, who were surprised and completely engaged, not by the artworks but by the noise and technology of the air conditioning. The teachers rapidly shifted their gaze to that as well, enabling creative conversations in the two museums. A number of writers have extolled the value of imagination in education: we include two more of them, Elliot Eisner and Vivian Gussin Paley. Elliot Eisner, an artist himself, was an eloquent and passionate advocate for imagination in education. He argued that the ability to remember without the ability to imagine would leave us with a static culture, and that imagining should be one of the basics of education: "to create new images, images that function in the development of a new science, the creation of a new symphony, and the invention of a new bridge" (Eisner, 2005, pp. 107–108). He describes people with imagination as "boundary breakers" who reject accepted assumptions, make the "given" problematic, and imagine new possibilities.

Imagination and play have also been a theme in Vivian Gussin Paley's teaching and writing for many years. Her books form a major research project into imagination, play, identity and creative storying. She recognised that early childhood and school classrooms can be a safe place to construct and re-run imaginative stories that have personal and, frequently, collective, meaning. In Paley's early years' classrooms, dramatic play—with the children as authors, directors, and players—enables children to explore sense-making and to recognise events, making the connection between imagination and resilience. In *The Girl with the Brown Crayon* (1997), Paley's class spend much of the year exploring the books of one author, Leo Lionni, and she writes about how children use imaginative stories to shape their lives.

> If readiness for school has meaning, it is to be found first in the children's flow of ideas, their own and those of their peers, families, teachers, books, and television, from play into story and back into more play. It was when I asked the children to dictate their stories and bring them to life again on a stage that the connections between play and analytical thinking became clear. The children and I were nourishing the ground and opening the seed packets, ready to plant our garden of ideas and identities.
> (Paley, 2004, p. 11)

E waihanga ana—Imagining at Mana Tamariki

Okatia, the pou (carved post, representing Okatia's journey), created by the tamariki

Kiimai	Pirangi au i ngā putiputi. He pai ki a Okatia ngā putiputi.	I want to have flowers because Okatia likes flowers.
Rāwhiti	Ka hoatu he hue ki runga i te pou. Tēra pea ka tuhi, ka peita rānei.	We can put a gourd on the pou. Maybe we can draw or paint it on.
Kaiako	He aha te take o te hue?	What is the purpose of the gourd?
Rāwhiti	Kia tau tōna mauri i tana haerenga.	To settle the energy during the journey. ("Energy" here is the life essence that is imbued in all living things at the time of the creation of those things. Well-being is expressed in mauri ora—thriving life essence—but the mauri can languish without proper care or if rituals are not carried out in an appropriate way).
Kiimai	Me tētahi ahi hoki.	We should have a fire too.
Kaiako	He aha te take o te ahi i te rākau?	Why would we have a fire on a tree?
Kiimai	Kia mahana a Okatia.	So that Okatia can be warm.
Kiimai	He mīharo a Okatia.	Okatia is special.
Te Pakaka	Me whakapiri i ngā toka me te kāpia, he rite ki ngā toka e rere ana i te wā i pātukituki ia i ngā pae maunga.	We should glue rocks on like how the rocks fly when he busts through the mountains.
Kiimaii	Me whai hoki i tētahi awa. He awa roa mai i raro ki runga rawa.	Then we need to have a river. A long river that goes from the bottom to the top.

The kaiako facilitates a meeting with the group of children where they identify what they need to create the pou (the carved post, representing Okatia's journey) and who might help them achieve their objective. Some of the ideas put forward by the children are to utilise a large cylinder that could be decorated by painting, drawing, tracing and glueing collage material. They begin to plan what they want to be represented on the pou and they sketch their ideas. The following are some examples documented from one of their initial planning meetings.

While creating the pou, the children face various challenges and need to find solutions. Rawhiti transitions from the idea of painting an outline of a gourd and koru (spiral design) to filling in the lines with black colour. This is his solution when the paint pen draws a wider line than he plans and there is not enough room left for the koru. He leaves frustrated that day and returns the next with his solution. Kiitahi is challenged to transfer the wheku (a representation of a human face, usually carved) onto the pou. She asks an older child to draw it for her. He recalls a skill he has learned previously, using tracing paper, and he models this strategy for Kiitahi who then traces the wheku onto the pou. Halfway through the project, the kaiako holds a meeting and asks the children where they will display the pou as it is too tall for their classroom. During this phase, the children discuss the possibility of exhibiting their pou at the museum alongside the carved pou of Okatia that is permanently installed there. The tamariki then host a meeting with the parents and elders in our community who they believe might be able to help or advance their goal to exhibit at the museum. The kaiako (teacher) then works with the children to create a video application seeking approval from the museum to exhibit the pou there. Here is some dialogue from the video:

Kaiako (teacher)	He aha e hiahia ai koe ki te kawe atu ki Te Manawa?	Why did you want to take it to Te Manawa?
Kiimai	Ki kitea e ngā mātua. Nā te mea kāore au i pirangi kia pakaru. Me tiaki. Me hoatu he taiapa kia kore tētahi e pā.	So that our parents could see it. And because I don't want it to be damaged. It must be looked after. We need to put a fence around it to prevent access to those who are not allowed to touch it.
Kiitahi	Kia kitea e te tokomaha. Kia ako rātou i ngā korero o Okatia.	So, lots of people could see it and learn the story of Okatia.

62 E Waihanga Ana: Imagining

They reflect on the process they used to create the pou, and the kaiako records the following:

Makahuri	He tino roa te wā ki te whakarite, engari he mahi tino pai ki au.	It was a really long process to create it but also very enjoyable.
Rawhiti	He nui ngā mea i whakaritea.	There was a lot to prepare.
Kiitahi	He mahi uaua i ētahi wā.	Sometimes it was difficult.
Kiimai	Pirangi au i ngā putiputi. He pai ki a Okatia ngā putiputi.	I want to have flowers because Okatia likes flowers.
Rāwhiti	Ka hoatu he hue ki runga i te pou. Tēra pea ka tuhi, ka peita rānei.	We can put a gourd on the pou. Maybe we can draw or paint it on.
Kaiako	He te take o te hue?	What is the purpose of the gourd?
Rāwhiti	Kia tau tōna mauri i tana haerenga.	To settle the energy during the journey.
Kiimai	Me tētahi ahi hoki.	We should have a fire too.
Kaiako	He aha te take o te ahi i te rākau?	Why would we have a fire on a tree?
Kiimai	Kia mahana a Okatia.	So that Okatia can be warm.
Kiimai	He mīharo a Okatia.	Okatia is special.
Te Pakaka	Me whakapiri i ngā toka me te kāpia, he rite ki ngā toka e rere ana i te wā i pātukituki ia i ngā pae maunga.	We should glue rocks on like how the rocks fly when he busts through the mountains.
Kiimai	Me whai hoki i tētahi awa. He awa roa mai i raro ki runga rawa.	Then we need to have a river. A long river that goes from the bottom to the top.

This project began at the Manawatū Gorge and then extends to the local museum where the tamariki think about creating their own artwork. During that process, they begin to imagine exhibiting the work, first at school and then at the local museum. With each stage of the project comes new understandings and additional ideas. Imagining is happening throughout the process, not just at the start. The local museum displayed the children's pou for a month.

Kaitiakitanga (trusteeship)

In this example, the children are carrying out their role as kaitiaki (trustees) by taking responsibility together to create a culturally significant project. They remained open to possibilities, and this allowed for an organic process that responds to and welcomes new ideas, challenges, understandings and experiences. They are collaboratively problem finding and problem solving with a clear purpose in mind. In this way, the children are able to be visionary as part of their duty as trustees and to make decisions in the interest of the collective.

E waihanga ana—Imagining at Tai Tamariki

Sarah's dinosaur drawings

Sarah draws one of the very large dinosaurs in the exhibition, adding an imaginative flourish in response to the kaiako describing it as "scary"[3].

During a visit to the dinosaur exhibition, Sarah looks around one of the exhibit rooms. A glass case that encloses a skeletal dinosaur head captures her attention and she runs towards it. The teacher who is accompanying her points out two dinosaur bones from a *triceratops horridus* that are on display beside the head. The teacher asks, "Do you want to have a touch, you're allowed to touch these (dinosaur bones)". Sarah hesitates and the teacher touches the bones. Then on tiptoes, Sarah, somewhat reluctantly, runs her hands along the larger leg bone. She tries to pick it up but its weighty resistance surprises her and she finds she can't lift it. She says "It's too heavy to lift it". She sits on the floor, gets out her clipboard and begins to draw the leg bone shape. Part way through making the oval shape she gets up and taps the bone with her pencil, reappraising its solidity perhaps, and rehearsing her earlier touching. Having done this, she sits down and completes the bone drawing then transforms it into a drawing of a dinosaur by adding a head with a smiley face and three legs each with four toes (Figure 5.1).

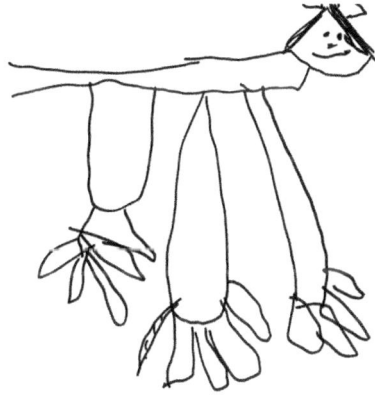

Figure 5.1 Sarah's drawing of the smiling dinosaur.

This interaction continues with the teacher's comment:

T: Friendly looking dinosaur you've got there Sarah [she laughs].
S: It's *not*! It's a scary dinosaur.
T: Really? It's got such a smiley face. Is that to make you, is that to trick people?
S: Yes.
T: They go "Oh that's a friendly dinosaur" and next minute, it goes "Rrrrrrr" [quiet roar sound]?
S: And now I'm going to do a witch's hat.
T: [Sitting down beside her.] "Holy moly, where's the witch come into it, why a witch?"
S: The witch is, the [She looks around and sees a brochure with a ferocious-looking dinosaur on the cover. She holds it up and adds] "This is a scary dinosaur, it's like this one".
T: Ahmm, so is the witch going to meet the dinosaur? Is that why?
S: This is the dinosaur and he's going to have a witch hat on it. [Sarah draws the "hat" on her picture of the dinosaur.] It's a, it's a witch, it's a dinosaur witch. [Sarah acts out being the dinosaur witch—sitting up on her knees, holding her arms up and bending her hands and fingers in a "scary" pose].

Later, when they returned to the kindergarten, Sarah dictated a description to be written by the teachers alongside this drawing in her drawing book: "It's a dinosaur walking with a witch hat on that looks like a flower but it's actually a witch's hat" (Figure 5.2).

In this sequence, Sarah's drawing in a correspondence with the teacher as reader co-produced an ambiguity and contradiction: the smiley face Sarah drew is a meme, or cultural image, for happy and friendly. However, Sarah firmly rejected this storyline: "It's not! It's a scary dinosaur". She reappraised her drawing and added a witch's hat, another cultural meme, to better reflect the dinosaur's character as being scary. She called on a brochure that depicted a ferocious dinosaur to assist her in convincing the teacher—her dinosaur—was scary. Earlier in the visit, the teacher had apologised to the children that there were pens only, not pencils, for drawing. Pens insist on a drawing as final product—any change will be a carrying-on, not an erasure.

Sarah's disguise

On a second occasion when Sarah visits the dinosaur exhibition, before she leaves the kindergarten, she stuffs a carry bag with pieces of fabric

E Waihanga Ana: Imagining 65

Figure 5.2 Sarah's drawing of the witch's hat.

from the "dress-up" corner. When she arrives at the museum exhibition, she puts the bag onto the floor and tells Becs, the accompanying teacher: "I want to put a costume on". She selects some of the material and drops the pieces of fabric she has chosen in a pile on the floor in the exhibition hall.

Becs: Is this the pile of things you are using?
Sarah: Yeah, and can you, where's the tummy one?
Becs: The tummy one? (looks through the pile) Is it like a waistband that you'd like to put around your waist? What about this? (selects a piece and holds it up)
Sarah: Yes ... .
Becs: (Checks on the purpose of this). So, you have something in mind Sarah? Have you thought about this before we came? (Becs holds up the largest piece) "This one?"
Sarah: Yes.
[The fabric is wrapped around Sarah, secured by the "tummy one". A few loose cut strips hang down.]

Becs: You've got tentacles again! [a reference to an earlier visit to the museums's giant squid, when Sarah made herself a Giant Squid costume].

On this occasion, when she waves the cut strips about, the teacher suggests that she is "an octopus". Sarah finds another piece and wants three holes to be cut out of it "Like a ghost".

Becs reminds Sarah that they didn't bring scissors.

Becs: What part of your body were you wanting to put it on?
Sarah: Head.

They turn it into a wide headband-type arrangement.

Sarah moves to an interactive screen on which there are animated dinosaurs interacting with the people who stand in front of it. She pulls the fabric down over her face, like a visor, so that "they" (the dinosaurs) "can't see me". "I'm not an octopus" … "No. I'm a, I'm a, I'm a, I'm a peek-a-boo". … She raises and pulls down the fabric over her face, each time with a little jump. "Peek-a-boo! ….." Sarah pushes the fabric up off her face and looks at the dinosaurs on the screen. She then pulls it down again: "Hello, hello!" (Bends her knees, stomps her feet. "I'm stomping like they do"). There is some discussion as to whether the dinosaurs are "scared" when she pushes the fabric down—like a mask (or a "ghost"?). The group moves on.

In this example, the materiality has been imaginatively crafted and invented by the child, Sarah. The costume and the visor have constructed a material anchoring for her storying, enabling her to *be in charge* of when and how she will look at, relate to or connect with, the rather ferocious dinosaur. The teacher, Becs, is familiar with Sarah's imaginative creations and prepared to collaborate: as a provider of materials for Sarah's imaginative purpose, and to make suggestions. Sarah did not appear to have the "peek-a-boo" visor in mind at the beginning; the fabrics of different sizes, and the absence of scissors to shape them for purpose, determined the materiality that led to an unscripted and imaginary scenario.

Trusteeship (kaitiakitanga)

For a description of the trusteeship in this example, we quote a reviewer of Vivian Paley's book, *A Child's Work: The importance of fantasy play*. Vivian Paley: Making the connection between imagination and resilience, to "plant our garden of ideas and identities":

Here, Paley mounts an eloquent and prophetic defence of creative time and fantasy play against the developers moving in to destroy the wetlands and forests of childhood in the name of standardized test preparation and easily measurable results.
(Joseph Featherstone in Paley, 2004, back cover)

Notes

1 Greene (2001). The chapter referenced here is a 1997 paper by Greene and included in her 2001 book.
2 A publication entitled Vision Mātauranga: Unlocking the Innovation Potential of Māori Knowledge, Resources and People (2007) from the (Aotearoa New Zealand) Ministry of Research, Science and Technology includes the following Mission Statement (p. 1): "To unlock the innovation potential of Māori knowledge, resources and people to assist New Zealanders to create a better future". One of the ambitions is (p. 22) "encouraging a spirit of creativity".
3 This story was first published in *Children's Geographies*. Authors: Margaret Carr, Jeanette Clarkin-Phillips, Brenda Soutar, Leanne Clayton, Miria Wipaki, Rea Wipaki-Hawkins, Bronwen Cowie & Shelley Gardner (Carr et al., 2018).

References

Carr, M., Clarkin-Phillips, J., Soutar, B., Clayton, L., Wipaki, M., Wipaki-Hawkins, R., Cowie, B., & Gardner, S. (2018). Young children's museum geographies: Spatial, material and bodily ways of knowing. *Children's Geographies*, *16*(5), 558–570. 10.1080/14733285.2018.1480750

Csiksentmihalyi, M. (1990). *Creativity: Flow and the psychology of discovery and invention*. HarperCollins.

Eisner, E. (2005). The John Dewey lecture of 2002. In E. W. Eisner (Ed.), *Reimagining schools: The selected works of Elliot W. Eisner* (pp. 205–214). Routledge.

Getzels J. W., & Csikszentmihalyi, M. (1975). From problem solving to problem finding. In I. A. Taylor & J. W. Getzels (Eds.), *Perspectives in creativity* (pp. 90–116). Aldine Publishing Company.

Greene, M. (2001). *Variations on a blue guitar: The Lincoln Centre Institute lectures on aesthetic education*. Teachers College Press.

Matamua, R. (2017). *Matariki. The star of the year*. Huia.

Meier, D. (1995) *The power of their ideas: Lessons for America from a small school in Harlem*. Beacon Press.

Meier, D. (2002). *In schools we trust: Creating communities of learning in an era of testing and standardisation*. Beacon Press.

MoRST. (2007). *Vision mātauranga. Unlocking the innovation potential of Maori knowledge, resources and people*. Ministry of Research, Science and Technology. https://www.mbie.govt.nz/info-services/science-innovation/agencies-policies-budget-initiatives/vm-booklet.pdf

Paley, V. G. (1997). *The girl with the brown crayon.* Harvard University Press.
Paley, V. G. (2004). *A child's work.* University of Chicago Press.
Sennett, R. (2008). *The craftsman.* Penguin Books.
Wenger, E. (1998). *Communities of practice: Learning, meaning, and identity.* Cambridge University Press.
Wertsch, J. V. (2002). *Voices of collective remembering.* Cambridge University Press.

6 E Whakaahua Ana: Using Multiple Modes

The use of traditional storytelling, arts and legends and of humour, proverbs and metaphoric language can support children from some communities to navigate between familiar and less familiar contexts. (Ministry of Education, 2017, p. 41)	*Mode* is the name for a culturally and socially fashioned resource for representation and communication. Mode has material aspects, and it bears everywhere the stamp of past cultural work. (Kress, 2004, p. 45)

Tim Ingold (2018) makes a connection between the arts and anthropology when he asks the following question: "Are artists the real anthropologists?"

He explains:

> Joining with the forces that give birth to ideas and things, rather than seeking to express what is already there, art that is anthropological conceives without being conceptual. Such art rekindles care and longing, allowing knowledge to grow from the inside of being in the correspondences of life. This is why such practices as walking, drawing, calligraphy, instrumental music, dance, ways of making and working with materials—ways that keep getting bracketed at the 'craft' end of the spectrum—are exemplary for me.

Giving thought room to breathe

In the early childhood contexts, when tamariki were deeply engaged in art and construction activities of their own choice, they were able at the same time to do some of the specific thinking that multi-modality enables. Tim Ingold (2018) noticed how one particular practice—taking a walk—focuses the mind in a special way: "Perhaps the meditative power of walking lies in precisely this: that it gives *thought room to breathe* (our emphasis), to let the world in on its reflections.... We must become responsive beings. Thus, even as I walk, I must adjust my footing to the terrain, follow the path, submit to the elements. There is, in every step, an element of uncertainty" (p. 23). And we note—from our descriptions in previous chapters of creative capacity building in action—that a particular practice could also focus the children's minds in a special way, and give them "thought room to breathe" in unique ways. Here are some examples in three earlier chapters that appear to illustrate teachers and kaiako giving young children visiting a museum "thought room to breathe":

- In Chapter 3, the kaiako (teacher) chatted to Rakei te Kura during a visit from Mana Tamariki to the local museum. As they watched an artist constructing an exhibit; he was shy about asking questions. Early in the visit, she said "Patai atu. Kia kaha" ("Ask him. Be courageous"). Rakei te Kura then began to ask questions, and an exploratory conversation began with the artist. In the dinosaur exhibition, Jack was given permission to return to the meteor exhibit when Tai Tamariki visited the museum. His familiarity with the purpose of the exhibit gave him room for re-enacting a thoughtful, sympathetic and creative re-enactment.
- In Chapter 4, Taumaihiroa, from Mana Tamariki, was given many opportunities to visit and sketch the museum's *mana aute* (traditional kite). This enabled her to creatively introduce her own cultural themes: incorporating Tawhirimatea (Māori god of the winds) and Tamanuiterā (the sun).
- Andrea, one of the teachers, "changes the scale" at Tai Tamariki. This reduced the anxiety, and enabled the interest and curiosity to breathe.
- In Chapter 5, the children at Mana Tamariki are collaboratively constructing a model of the pou and discuss what Okatia would need on the journey. This was an opportunity, taken up enthusiastically by the tamariki (children), to cooperate and to share ideas and skills. It also led to an imaginatively constructed video request to the museum by Taioperua (this chapter).

Sarah makes two drawings of dinosaurs during a Tai Tamariki visit to the local museum. She "holds the pen" and is thus in charge of responding to the teacher's suggestion that this is a "friendly" dinosaur. She changes her drawing, to better represent her thinking when she first drew the dinosaur as "scary".

Connection with Reggio Emilia

Across many generations, Māori have been skilled in a wide range of communication and storying modes—not having in traditional times a written script, gifted orators and artists could—and can now—shift from one mode to another to tell and retell stories: te reo (the Māori language), waiata (song), karakia (ritual acknowledgements), whaikōrero (speech-making), oriori (lullabies), carving and weaving, for instance, when the occasion called. It is not surprising therefore that Mana Tamariki developed a strong interest in the philosophy of multi-modal affordances eloquently expressed and exemplified in action by the teachers and artists at Reggio Emilia in northern Italy (see commentary by Loris Malaguzzi, 1994, and Carlina Rinaldi, 2006). Kaiako at Mana Tamariki value the multi-modal philosophy in the Italian Reggio Emilia schools and have drawn upon their ideas to enhance their kaupapa Māori approach and, especially, to build on their own multi-modal repertoire. The notion of "a hundred languages" in Reggio resonated with their view of learning as did the Reggio view of the "environment as the third teacher". Since 1999, kaiako have participated in professional development study tours of Reggio philosophies in Melbourne and Reggio Emilia. As Carlina Rinaldi (an executive consultant for Reggio Children and a professor at the University of Modena and Reggio) has commented: "Creativity is not just the quality of thinking of each individual but is also an interactive, relational and social project. It requires a context that allows it to exist, to be expressed, to become visible.... What we hope for is creative learning and creative teachers, not just a 'creative hour'" (2006, pp. 119–120). Gunilla Dahlberg and Peter Moss remember (in an introduction to that 2006 Rinaldi book, p. 7) that Loris Malaguzzi talked about the idea of knowledge in the Reggio Emilia schools as a "tangle of spaghetti"; they also remind the readers of Carlina's commentary that "learning does not proceed in a linear way, determined and deterministic". Rather, the project work in Reggio can be seen as "a series of small narratives, narratives that are difficult to combine in an additive and cumulative way". In Chapters 7 and 8, we suggest ways to connect the coordinates together, and to hazard some ideas about how the small narratives from Mana Tamariki and Tai Tamariki might be able to "carry on".

E whakaahua ana—Using multiple modes at Mana Tamariki

We look back at the examples in previous chapters, for both sites, to note the multiple modes within the compass of creative storying.

At Mana Tamariki, examples included imagining a new kupu (word); drawing an exhibit in a sketch book; paintings; dancing, drawing and explaining manu aute (traditional kites); multiple modes during the construction of a pou; creating a video; and group discussions. At Tai Tamariki, they included drama (the children devising a production); embodied representation (of a meteor destroying the dinosaurs); manipulating with fabric; using fabrics as a disguise, drawing, and cardboard construction. In all the early years settings, the teachers and the resources offered children opportunities to represent their interests in a variety of modes. In all sites, resources were readily available to assist the meaning-making. These interests in, and opportunities for, combining modes may be a common quality of education in the early years; it has lessons for education in all the sectors, including the university. In this chapter, we elaborate on Gunther Kress's (2004) comment: "I want to say that meanings, in the broad sense, can be realised in any mode, but that when they are, they are realised in mode-specific articulations" (p. 107).

Here, from Mana Tamariki, is an example where the mode described is "walking the land" in a landscape of cultural significance for the Mana Tamariki community. Here is a paki ako (learning story) that refers to this event, written in te reo Māori by one of the kaiako (teachers); it was added to all the children's portfolios, and translated for this book.

> The places my feet have walked
> Te Aurere-a-te-Tonga (a spiritual being that lives in the Manawatu Gorge), call us here!
> Here Mana Tamariki prepares to view your exhibition.

Tamariki, last year we began to engage more deeply with the Manawatū river. This year we are broadening our knowledge of the region by trekking through this place we live. We commenced this morning with a walk into The Gorge. This is the gorge that Okatia shaped as she/he (*note the Māori word for she/he is gender neutral*) travelled from the slopes of the Puketoi ranges to the Tasman Ocean. Far on in time, the ancestor Hau took his famous journey where he named the river, Manawatū. These are the stories we concentrated on last year. But, did you know that The Gorge is a most unique area? It is the only place in New Zealand and the Southern Hemisphere where a river flows from one side of the mountain range to the opposite side. Perhaps our investigation over the next few weeks will help us to understand why the Manawatū river is like this.

The story of Okatia had been passed down intergenerationally within the local iwi (tribe), and the kaiako (teachers) create experiences for tamariki (children) to engage with the pūrākau (story) by retelling the story in various ways, including reading books, excursions to the river, gorge and mountains, museum visits, watching short movies, participating in performing arts and viewing different artworks. Children express their thoughts and ideas in many different modes. Kiitahi painted Okatia and the Manawatu River. Te Pakaka pulls a long weed from the garden. He places it in the sandpit and digs a pathway that he fills with water retelling the story as he does so. Taumaihiroa makes a tree and two mountains out of playdough. She re-enacts the story using the playdough figures. All the tamariki sketched pictures and paintings on numerous occasions. In Chapter 5, as noted earlier in this chapter, the class as a whole created a pou (the carved post) depicting the story of Okatia.

That pou construction was an example of the children using multiple modes to achieve the task they had set; it included a variety of art activity, for example, painting, drawing, tracing and glueing collage material, but it also references the diverse ways the children explored their ideas. This included digital documentation, formal meetings and discussions and casual conversations. The role of the kaiako to assist the children towards their aspirations is also realised by the kaiako listening, observing and providing challenges, questions, reflections and support, enabling the children to progress their idea.

A *kaitiaki (trustee)* in the Māori world is required to make meaning using a range of modes that can include listening, observing, formal speech-making, leading meetings, upholding spiritual and ceremonial rituals and creating taonga (artefacts) with natural resources through weaving and other forms of art. This multi-modal approach is carried out in various contexts across the traditional and modern worlds, spiritual and physical realms and in known and unknown spaces. Through the Okatia project, the children were able to use multiple modes to build their creative capacities. They constructed the *pou* (in Chapter 5) that tells the story of Okatia's journey and produced a

74 E Whakaahua Ana: Using Multiple Modes

video of this construction as part of an application to have their *pou* included in the museum's exhibitions. Taioperua was the producer; here is another paki ako (learning story), translated into English for this book, about this work.

> Taioperua, The Producer
>
> What an awesome idea you had to create a short film showing the story of Okatia.
>
> You also wanted to broadcast te reo Māori on YouTube, to the world.
>
> I was amazed watching you leading your friends, delegating the picture drawing, taking photos and the haka (a fierce dance, often a challenge to or for another or others). You carefully selected who you were going to ask by the skills of your friends. You asked Ihaka and Rāwhiti to voice record the haka of Okatia.
>
> I was overwhelmed with joy to know that you knew the skills and talents of your friends.
>
> Nau i whatu te kakahu, he taniko taku,
> Yours is the useful work, mine ornamental

Te Koha (a six-year-old) and a karakia (a mode of speech, in te reo, as an acknowledgement).

Also written up as a paki ako (learning story):

Nāku Koe e Tama.	I am proud of you.
Te Koha, i te hokinga atu ki Te Āpiti inanahi ka puta koutou ngā Tūngoungou i te waka mau ka hui ki te tomokanga.	Te Koha, when we returned to the Gorge yesterday, your Tūngoungou group got out of the van and went to the entranceway.
I a au e whakarite ana i ngā pīkau ka rangona tō reo rangatira.	As I was getting the backpacks ready, I heard the Māori language recited.
"Nau mai e ngā hua o te wao, o te ngakina, o te waitai, o te wai Māori. Nā Tāne, nā Rongo, nā Tangaroa, nā Maru. Ko Ranginui e tū iho nei, ko Papatūānuku e takoto ake nei. Turuturu o whiti whakamaua kia tina! Haumi e, hui e, taiki e!"	This is a karakia, an acknowledgement recited before partaking of food. It is a direct address to relevant gods.

(Continued)

Te Koha, i mōhio koe ka tukuna ngā mihi, ngā whakaaro nui i mua i te kuhunga ki Te Āpiti. Māhau, mā Rangitāne mātou e arahī ka tika.

Ahakoa he ruruku kai kē tāu, i mīharo au ki te hononga o te ruruku i kōwhiritia me taku mōhio ko tērā atu, ko "Taumaha tini ki runga nei ..." kē te ruruku e auau nei te puta i tō waha.

He mahi nui whakahirahira te karakia, te ruruku, te tuku mihi e tūhonohono ai te rangi ki te whenua, te whenua ki te rangi, ā, ko ngā mea katoa i waenganui.

Ko tō mahi inanahi e whakaū ana i tō mōhio ki ngā tikanga me kawe, ahakoa he ruruku kai kē tāu. Kua whakaatu mai koe kei te mōhio koe me karakia i mua i te urunga atu. He tamaiti Māori koe e tipu ana i roto i te reo Māori, i ngā tikanga Māori hoki.

He ata koe nā ō tīpuna, heke, heke ki ērā o ō kaumātua, te hunga kua riro mā rātou ngā mahi nei e waha i tēnei, tō koutou rohe. Kia kaha matou, ō kaiwhakaako, ki te maimoa i a koe i roto i ēnei mahi.

He koanga ngākau te kite i a koe e pakeke haere ana hei raukura mō ō iwi.

Te Koha, you knew that acknowledgements should be offered before entering the Gorge. It was up to you because you are Rangitāne, the local tribal group connected to this land and it is for you to lead us.

Although you offered an acknowledgement for food, I was impressed that you selected that particular food acknowledgement because the other popular acknowledgement is "Taumaha tini ki runga nei ..." and that is what is usually selected.

Ritual acknowledgements are an important practice connecting the sky to the earth, earth to sky and everything between.

What you did yesterday confirmed that you know how to uphold rituals even though it was an acknowledgement of the food you selected. What you showed was your understanding that a ritual needed to be completed before entering the bush walk. You are a Māori child growing up speaking Māori and upholding Māori ways of being and doing.

You are a reflection of your ancestors, coming down, down to your grandparents, to the ones that are carrying these traditions in this region where you belong. We, your teachers, must support and nurture you in all these tasks.

I recognise with joy your achievement today as you move towards your role as a high achiever who exemplifies the hopes and aspirations of your people.

E whakaahua ana—Using multiple modes at Tai Tamariki

Examples from Tai Tamariki of multiple modes were described in Chapter 5, where Sarah drew a dinosaur, and in response to a challenge from a teacher, changing the narrative to better reflect her interpretation and intention. Later in that chapter, she used scraps of fabric to construct a disguise, as a "ghost", possibly to enable her to be in charge of her relationship with the big dinosaur model. The modes—drawing and disguising—changed the effect.

Andrea's planning book

In Chapter 4, Andrea had described her introduction of fabrics and puppetry to create opportunities for creative storying at Tai Tamariki kindergarten and to "change the scale"—also to change the effect, to enable one of the boys to be less scared of the dinosaur exhibits. Here, we add her comments about drawing in a Planning Book, modelling for the children the value of drawing as a way to "make sense" as well as claiming it as a useful mode for the children.

Andrea: I've kind of got in the habit of drawing things down because I do that myself, I didn't used to do it with the children but I do now … .

Margaret: Do you? Draw plans with the children?

Andrea: Yeah, I just draw them while they're playing and then one (of the children) will come and say "What are you doing?" and then I'll say "I'm putting it in the teacher's planning book" and it's quite good because then we can go back a few weeks because it's every five weeks I'm out there (on duty outside). I can look back to five weeks ago and we can talk about what we did. I've done a bit of work with Hunter, drawing constructions, so that he can see the design process and use it. So, I've got into the habit of whenever I have an idea and I'm working through it I just jot it down. And so, Gia added her bit there as well.

Margaret: (Looking at the page) What does it say?

Andrea: "It's a dinosaur but now it's a turtle". She changed it; she wanted to add to it so I often end up with these pages (in her Planning Book) that have got their drawings next to it.

Rose constructs an alasaurus

Lou, a teacher at Tai Tamariki, writes up this event:

> While setting up the small dinosaurs with Peter P we talked about what their names were. We both didn't know so I asked Peter P to go and look for a dinosaur book. He came back with one, then we started looking at the pictures to identify the dinosaurs and when we did, I wrote the names on the dinosaurs. While we were talking about it, Rose arrived. Rose was interested in dinosaurs and she set off to make one. She split an egg carton in half, then cleverly arched the egg part backwards (creating a spine) then arched it onto the other half of the tray, calling "Can you help me Lou?". I held onto the bits while Rose sellotaped it. Many times, the sellotape came off and we had to find the edge. While aiding Rose to make her dinosaur it attracted other tamariki to make one. We talked while we were making our creations and the rich conversations spurred the tamariki ideas. "What is the name of your dinosaur Rose?" Rose: "Pointasaurus"—which she later changed into Alsasaurus (which is no big guess why: Alsa from 'Frozen', a popular film). Rose took her dinosaur to show at the morning mat time and more tamariki wanted to make one.
>
> Rose, what a brilliant idea you had, you were able to explain your ideas and I had fun sitting alongside you. You even thought about how to care for the dinosaur by making some juice.

Rose dictates a story, enabling a reviewing by using photos to anchor the conversation and the critique

In this second example, Rose is dictating a Learning Story to the teacher about her visit to the dinosaur exhibition. She was trying to make sense of the movement of parts of the museum exhibit, in this case, a shadow that seemed to be out of sync with the physical model. One of the teachers invites her to make some comments alongside photos taken during the visit. Rose and the teacher are back at the kindergarten, looking at the photos on the computer screen. Rose wants to make a statement that will be recorded. Here is part of their conversation.

Rose: I think you should get it bigger so I can see what's happening.
Teacher: (Enlarges the pictures) Can you see it now?

Rose: Yes (referring to the first photo) I am microphoning you.
Teacher: You asked me to give it (the microphone) to you so you could say something in it. Do you remember what you wanted to say into the microphone?
Rose: (Dictates) I went to the dinosaur exhibition and I said in the microphone that the dinosaur claw looks like an elephant's tooth. Because at K. (another centre she has been to) I saw something that a kid's dad told me that it's an elephant's tooth.

One skeleton had a shadow and one didn't. One moved and one didn't and I don't know how that happened. One had a projector and one didn't have a projector. Well, see this T-Rex here (pointing to one of the photographs), it has a shadow and it looks like this one here doesn't.

The creative addition to Rose's dictated story was to make an analogy between the dinosaur claw and an elephant's tooth, calling on a remembered conversation. Maybe this can be described as an "analytical" "material blend". The technology for a shadow display of two skeletal dinosaurs (one moving, and one still) was what she especially noticed and found puzzling and "illogical" (but not, apparently, "scary"). For her, this raised an ambiguity or a problem. In both Tai Tamariki and Mana Tamariki, children often dictated at least some words for their narrative assessment portfolios. Teachers transcribed their contributions carefully, enabling the children to refer to photographs and to read some of the words back to their families and whānau, enhancing the "going-on" of these learning episodes.

Further comments on giving thought room to breathe

Elliot Eisner (2005), in a book of his selected works, writes about the value of "Using forms of representation" as follows:

> This process of making the private public is a process we take too much for granted. It is an extraordinary achievement, one that is still evolving, and, though language is our prime vehicle, we have over time found it necessary to create other means through which what we have thought, felt and imagined could be given a public face (p. 108).

He adds (pp. 108–109) that the use of any form of representation has at least four important educational functions:

First, it is important to recognize that there is nothing so slippery as a thought. Working with a form of representation provides the opportunity to stabilize what is ephemeral and fleeting.

Second, it gives a student a way of holding on to their thinking (as, in this chapter, Taioperua recognised when he decided to produce a film, and Rose recognised when she dictated a learning story)

The third function of using a form of representation to externalise the internal is to make communication possible.

The fourth function (of particular interest in this book) is to provide opportunities for discovery. ... The creative act is an act of exploration and discovery.

We agree with Eisner (2005, p. 109) when he adds:

Thinking should be celebrated by giving students opportunities to try to represent what they think they know. And because what they think they know cannot always be projected in a single form of representation—say, the logical use of language—they should have a variety of options available and the skills with which to use them.

References

Eisner, E. (2005). *Reimagining schools: The selected works of Elliot W. Eisner*. Routledge.
Ingold. T. (2018). *Anthropology and/as education*. Routledge.
Kress, G. (2004). *Literacy in the new media age*. Routledge.
Malaguzzi, L. (1994). History, ideas and basic philosophy. In C. Edwards, L. Gandini & G. Forman (Eds.), *The hundred languages of children: The Reggio Emilia approach to early childhood education* (pp. 49–97). Ablex Publishing.
Ministry of Education. (2017). *Te Whariki: Early childhood curriculum*. https://www.education.govt.nz/assets/Documents/Early-Childhood/Te-Whariki-Early-Childhood-Curriculum-ENG-Web.pdf
Rinaldi, C. (2006). *In dialogue with Reggio Emilia: Listening, researching and learning*. Routledge.

7 He Taonga, He Rerenga Arorangi[1]

> The culture our ancestors brought with them was a taonga, a treasure. It was a taonga they have handed on to us. It was a taonga that we in turn add to and hand on. Our culture, our taonga, does not end with us. It goes on, on into the future.
> (Adsett et al., 2005, p. 14)

> I prefer to think of dispositions rather than skills because wise actions will not be produced spontaneously unless a person is disposed toward them, that is, inclined to see appropriate occasions and to act on them. To be wise, I think you have to be ready and willing as well as able.
> (Claxton, 2008, p. 35)

This book has connected cultural anchors with creativity dispositions. In Chapter 1, we noted Linda Tuhiwai Smith's comment that qualitative research seems to be "most able to weave and unravel competing (cultural) storylines", and in Chapter 2, we introduced four *Cultural Anchors* to anchor the different cultural storylines during these specific contexts: two different cultural storylines. In four coordinates chapters (Chapters 3–6), we described creative capacity building via the teaching and participant's observation during museum visits from the two early education sites: (i) Mana Tamariki kōhanga ki te kura (*ki tā te Māori titiro, ki ta te wairua Māori*, where only te reo Māori is spoken) and (ii) Tai Tamariki kindergarten (*pakeha and tauiwi*) where mostly English is spoken.

In this and Chapter 8, we describe creative capacity building via the Cultural Anchors introduced in Chapter 2:

1 We were gifted the title "he taonga, he rerenga arorangi": "where there are treasured objects the spirit will be nurtured and creativity will be inspired". This was Cultural Anchor 1, and unpacking this

title, with young children, museum visits and creative capacity building in mind is the task for this chapter.

2 In Chapter 8, we will return to Cultural Anchors 2, 3 and 4 to emphasise that, as a result of their museum experiences tamariki and children might become *kaitiaki* or *trustees*. However, in that chapter, we suggest that the kaitiakitanga and trusteeship will not only refer to the presence and preservation of the museum objects. It will especially refer to the *animating*: a "gathering of materials in movement", a "correspondence", whereby objects become "things", as Tim Ingold had proposed (2012 p. 427). This will finalise this discussion (but never end it) of "creative capacity building": ongoing storying and re-storying. We will outline three ongoing pathways that connect the material to the pedagogy and the children's responses, in order to explore these conclusions.

Applying the unifying framing—He taonga, he rerenga arorangi

In 1994, Mason Durie constructed an alignment of parameters of health for Māori in terms of a metaphor of a four-sided *health construct*, a four-sided *house* or *whare tapawhā* (Durie, 1994).[2] Here, we consider whether there is a similarly unifying construct that would embrace all four *creative capacity-building coordinates*.

For our gathering together, we highlight the first of the Cultural Anchors, an overarching perspective—*he taonga, he rerenga arorangi*—translated by the Mana Tamariki team as "Where there are treasured objects, the spirit will be nurtured and creativity will be inspired".

- The first frame is communities and places *where objects are treasured.*
- The second frame is where there are treasured objects, *the spirit will be nurtured.*
- The third frame is where there are treasured objects, the spirit will be nurtured and *creativity will be inspired.*

Treasuring the objects and the knowledge

A first frame to gather together the coordinates:

he taonga, he rerenga arorangi—communities and places *where objects are treasured* will be spaces where the spirit is nurtured.

At the outset of visits to the museum, the Mana Tamariki whānau gathered to hear a panel of tribal experts who are connected to the taonga talk about their aspirations for the relationship they themselves and visitors might grow and maintain with the objects. The panel was instrumental in guiding the way the kōhanga proceeded with the visits, how they carried out protocols, rituals and ceremonies; and how the objects would be cared for and treasured.

While at the Te Manawa Museum Rakei Te Kura (in Chapter 3) drew an exhibit, an ancestor with a hat and some jandals, representing the old and the new world. Brenda and Leanne explain that "Rakei Te Kura" is a member of the local tribe to whom the stories of local place belong. His genealogical connection to the Manawatū river, the mountain ranges and Okatia support his information gathering. Part of his role as a kaitiaki (trustee) is to maintain and protect the stories of his ancestors. In doing so, Rakei Te Kura strengthens his own identity and sense of belonging within the contemporary world that he exists. His picture of Rangimatua draws upon his encounter with the artist at the museum and gives context to his ideas about the old and new worlds. It is a drawing of the actual exhibit. This exhibit—and Rakei te Kura's drawing—illustrates an ancestor. The artwork illustrates a *whakapapa* of this ancestor, who is accompanied on his travels by a bird, a marae, a mountain, a tree, and a carved staff. Kaiako remind the tamariki that everything has a whakapapa, and that the ancestor is therefore responsible as a kaitiaki for this whakapapa. The story of this ancestor was a treasure, which would include all the four coordinates together (Figure 7.1).

Figure 7.1 Rangimatua: Drawing by Rakei Te Kura.

At Tai Tamariki, before every visit with the children, the kaiako visited the exhibition, researched the topic, shared their knowledge together, and found resources that would encourage the children's interest and recognition—in this case, for the dinosaur exhibition—that these are significant re-enactments of the treasured past. Some of the children also became the kindergarten's custodians of specialist knowledge, becoming familiar with narratives on this subject. For the dinosaur exhibition, the teachers collected together (from the kindergarten and the local library) relevant books, and this assisted the budding scientists and experts. The teachers knew that initially children would be afraid of the big dinosaur exhibits, so they began to counter that with conversations and scientific information at the children's level. Before the visits, one teacher had set small plastic dinosaurs in ice, and the children chipped away at this, learning about what "archaeologists" do, and checking the names of each dinosaur when they retrieved it.

Nurturing the spirit

A second frame to gather together the coordinates:

he taonga, he rerenga arorangi—where there are treasured objects there will be the freedom o soar to the heights of one's creative potential in a space where the spirit is nurtured.

Taking inspiration from the pou (carved post, illustrating Okatia's journey creating the Manawatu Gorge in Aotearoa New Zealand) at the museum, back at Mana Tamariki the children had decided to create their own (see Chapter 5). They planned the project from creation to exhibition. When the children's pou was unveiled for exhibition at the museum, an opening ceremony was held. The entire Mana Tamariki community was invited to attend, adding to the *mana* (prestige, power) of the occasion and confirming the significance of the children's achievement on behalf of the community. An example of the power of nurturing the spirit (as well as inspiring the creativity) was during the project when one of the children added a picture of a gourd to the children's pou; a kaiako asked what was the purpose for this. He replied "kia tau tona mauri i taua haerenga" (to settle the energy during the journey). The creativity continued after the children's conversations and the pou were completed. Taioperua worked on a request to the local Te Manawa Museum to display the children's pou there. He developed the request as a video production, directing individual tamariki to each make a contribution, recognising their individual talents and inclinations.

The dinosaur exhibition portrayed a storyline for the Tai Tamariki children that included very large model dinosaurs, moving dioramas, games, and interactive opportunities. Jack appeared to be particularly interested in the narrative of the dinosaurs' destruction, and this was illustrated in a part of the exhibition that provided a vivid portrayal of this: an interactive activity and a timeline diagram. During the visit (see Chapter 3), Jack returned to look again at a diagram that illustrated the timeline of the dinosaurs. He explains to Jeanette:

Jack: (*gestures to a timeline illustrated on the wall*) This is the ones where the dinosaurs, and here's some more dinosaurs on this.
Jeanette: So, what's this telling us?
Jack: This telling us which dinosaurs lived in the day of the dinosaurs (waves his hand over the timeline chart).

The vivid nature of the large model dinosaurs plus the opportunity for an embodied response—"the harder you jump, the bigger the meteor you create"—from Jack, and his gathering of information combined with the exhibit to provoke the (later) creative enactment of his response: acting out a dying dinosaur, describing it with an effect of sadness.

Inspiring the creativity

> *A third frame* to gather together the coordinates is implicit in *he taonga, he rerenga arorangi*—where there are treasured objects the spirit will be nurtured and (in a wise community) creativity will be inspired.

We have earlier described creative capacity-building events as an ecosystem in which the small references the big, a common role for artefacts and taonga in museum exhibitions. A version of this is the notion of a "common-good" perspective. We quote Anna Craft to explain:

> Studies by the research group at Harvard University known as the GoodWork project (working in conjunction with researchers at Stanford and Claremont universities) ... note a decreasing tendency to prioritize the *common-good* perspective among ambitious young people seeking to excel in three professions studied (journalism, science and acting) ... to see oneself as operating alone rather than as part of a community.
> (Craft, 2008, p. 29, our italics)

As a consequence of this, there is a challenge for educators in fostering the emergence of wisdom (i.e., taking account of multiple forms of understanding and knowledge) (Craft, 2008, p. 7). A *common-good*, wise, perspective can connect together information gathering, growing a relationship, imagining difference, and using multiple modes and literacies. Anna Craft (2008, p. 29)[3] argues for creativity in education to include nurturing a person's capacity to orient towards wisdom, as a *common-good perspective* rather than a more individualised and "self-centred" orientation. In Guy Claxton's (2008) words, writing about wisdom: "I prefer to think of dispositions rather than skills because wise actions will not be produced spontaneously unless a person is disposed towards them, that is, inclined to see appropriate occasions and to act on them. To be wise, I think you have to be ready and willing, as well as able" (p. 42). Other literature on learning dispositions in education, especially the writing and research led by David Perkins during Project Zero at Harvard University in the 1990s (Perkins et al., 1993), also described a learning disposition via that triangular format that describes a combination of (a) inclination (being ready), (b) a sensitivity to the occasion (being willing) and (c) ability (being able). Learning dispositions were introduced in Chapter 2. It is the "sensitivity to occasion" that takes a disposition and capacity into a sociocultural frame and links to children being empowered to have an opinion. It insists that the "occasion" includes (in addition to the objects) the opportunities, encouragements and invitations in the educational (and museum) environment that were central to the opportunities for children's creative capacities. It includes, for teachers, some curriculum-in-action imperatives. In the discussions from Mana Tamariki, this means central to *"growing raukura"*[4] (high achievers who exemplify the hopes and aspirations of their people) and central to *"creative capacity building"*.

Where might we find wisdom within creative capacity building for young children? This "common-good" community perspective gives creative storying and re-storying a wider meaning so that the whole is greater than the parts and "even very small objects become part of the wider context that gives them meaning", as Mason Durie had commented in a chapter based on an address to the World Heritage Committee's Pacific Workshop held at Turangi, New Zealand, in February 2007. These perspectives can apply in all the coordinates.

In Chapter 3 (e rangahau ana—information gathering) at Te Manawa museum, the encouragement from the kaiako and the artist's wisdom and generosity developed into a space that nurtured for Rakei te Kura an interest in the "stylish hip-hop" representation of a *tupuna* (in this case a mythical ancestor). The artist reminds him of the spiritual domain of mātauranga Māori, that "everything has a whakapapa (a genealogy and a cultural identity)". In Chapter 4 (e whakawhanaunga ana—growing a relationship), Tauimaihiroa responds to the exhibition of te manu, a traditional kite, animating it by her actions—in her drawing at every visit, and in her words—"Kei te rere ia ki te katoa o ngā wāhi". "She (the kite) is flying to all the places." In a sense, by creatively transposing ("playing" in a different key) the traditional Māori kite on display she was assisting the museum to create the kite exhibit as "a space where the spirit is nurtured". And, through her drawings, and her setting the scene with reference to the spiritual domains of Tamanuiterā (the sun god) and Tāwhirimātea (god of winds and storms), her creativity was inspired.

Chapter 4 also included creative capacity building—in a different way. This time it was illustrated back at the kindergarten by the teacher, and taken up by the children, to represent "moving" fabric dinosaurs. This inspired creativity reduced the anticipated fearful "spirit" of the dinosaur exhibits and enabled creative collaborations between teachers, children and taonga to coordinate the museum's messages about these amazing creatures.

While at the museum, in Chapter 5, Sarah is in charge of elaborating on an encounter with a fossilised dinosaur bone. She completes a drawing of a "smiley" dinosaur, and when the teacher challenges her: "Friendly looking dinosaur you've got there Sarah", she is indignant: "It's not! It's a scary dinosaur". She takes up the drawing again, and adds what she calls a "witch's hat". She then acts out being a dinosaur—sitting up on her knees, bending her arms and curling her fingers in a "scary" claw-like pose. During a later visit, fabrics are employed again. Sarah is inspired towards a further creative and playful re-authoring when she takes a bag of scrap material with her to the dinosaur museum and constructs a "disguise" while she is there. In that episode, teacher Becs became the assistant as Sarah constructed a costume that included a visor, enabling a "peek-a-boo" opportunity so that she was in charge of when she looked at the ferocious dinosaur. In Chapter 6, Gunther Kress (2003) reminded us that "meanings, in the broad sense, can be realised in any mode, but that when they are, they are realised in mode-specific articulations" (p. 107) (in this case, the *meaning* for Sarah was, perhaps, whakamana/empowerment, and the mode was a creative "disguise"). During the discussion of the museum's dinosaur museum exhibition, the children (in this case Jack, acting, and Sarah, drawing and disguising), and the teacher (using fabric puppetry) were realising their own mode-specific articulations that highlighted a possible, common *relational* good during a museum visit—an opportunity to be inventive, even during a "scary" exhibition—while still recognising the museum's narrative (Figures 7.2 and 7.3).

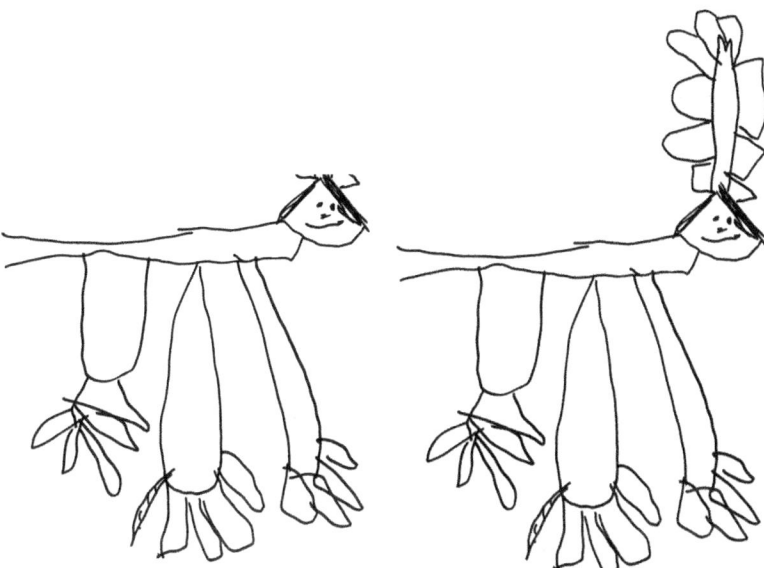

Figure 7.2 Sarah's drawing of the smiling dinosaur.

Figure 7.3 Sarah's drawing of the witch's hat.

The creative capacity building was shared by the tamariki, kaiako (including kaumatua and often whānau), and taonga. Together, and in different ways, this combination was treasuring the knowledge, nurturing the spirit, and inspiring the creativity. The builders of creative capacities connected the coordinates, and we return to the metaphor, introduced in chapter two, of the coordinates as stars that, separately and together, in an array-like Matariki, guided their travel—in this case, their creative capacity building. This way forward recognises that while museum exhibition developers were trustees/kaiako for treasured objects in the museum, and the teachers/kaiako recognised creative attitudes as being of great merit and were willing to work hard to support them, a powerful sub-text that emerged from the examples was that the *children and tamariki* during these visits were becoming apprentice *trustees for creative capacities*. This is a narrative that will be explored in Chapter 8.

Notes

1 This title was gifted to us from the Māori team. They translate it for us as: "Where there are treasured objects, the spirit is nurtured and creativity will be inspired".
2 Durie (1994). *Whaiora: Māori Health Development*, 2nd ed. Oxford: Oxford University Press. In this volume, he describes his original Whare Tapa Whā, a four-sided health construct later known as a whare whā (a four-sided house): Taha Wairua, Taha Hinengaro, Taha Tinana, Taha Whānau (Spiritual, Mental, Physical and Extended Family). Originally published as (1985) "A Māori Perspective of Health", *Journal of Social Sciences and Medicine 20* (5), 483–486.
3 We met Anna Craft in Chapter 2, calling for a cultural lens on creativity in education. She also writes a chapter entitled Tensions in Creativity and Education: Enter Wisdom and Trusteeship?: Chapter 2 in the 2008 book entitled *Creativity, Wisdom, and Trusteeship*, edited by Craft with Howard Gardner and Guy Claxton.
4 te tamaiti he raukura (high achievers who exemplify the hopes and aspirations of their people). See Chapter 2, Cultural Anchor 3.

References

Adsett, S., Whiting, C., Karetu, T., Lardelli, D., & Ihimaera, W. (2005). Mataora the living space. In S. Adsett & C. Whiting (Eds.), *Mataroa the living face: Contemporary Maori art, te waka toi*. Bateman.

Claxton, G. (2008). Wisdom: Advanced creativity? Chapter 3. In A. Craft, H. Gardner & G. Claxton (Eds.), *Creativity, wisdom and trusteeship*, (pp. 35–48). Corwin.

Craft, A. (2008). Tensions in creativity and education: Enter wisdom and trusteeship? In A. Craft, H. Gardner & G. Claxton (Eds.), *Creativity, wisdom and trusteeship: Exploring the role of education* (pp. 16–35). Corwin Press.

Durie, M. (1994). *Whaiora: Māori health development* (2nd ed.) Oxford University Press.

Ingold, T. (2012). Toward an ecology of materials. *Annual Review of Anthropology, 41*, 427–422. 10.114 6/annurev-anthro-081309-145920

Kress, G. (2003). *Literacy in the new media age*. Routledge.

Perkins, D., Jay, E., & Tishman, S. (1993). Beyond abilities: A dispositional theory of thinking. *Merrill-Palmer Quarterly, 39*(1), 1–21.

8 Creative Capacity Building: A Going On

> We should not thus think of the properties of materials as attributes. Rather they are histories.
> (Ingold, 2011, p. 32)
>
> To understand materials is to be able to tell their histories – of what they do and what happens to them when treated in particular ways – in the very practice of working with them. … They carry on, overtaking the formal destinations, that, at one time or another, have been assigned to them.
> (Ingold, 2012, p. 434, 435)

> In an indigenous world objects that appear to be inanimate are not regarded as lifeless or static since they also possess an identity of their own and are part of a wider network. Belonging to that network creates a vibrant relationship that is at odds with the view that motionless objects lack life. In the language of global warming and climate change, so-called inert objects may well have carbon credits that ultimately add to the world's equilibrium.
> (Durie, 2010, p. 243)

In this book, we have had in mind the ideas about creative capacity building as a "going on", from Tim Ingold and Mason Durie. In Chapter 7, we unpacked the title for this project to describe creative capacity building when young children visit museums—*he taonga, he rerenga arorangi*—(i) where there are objects that are treasured, and (ii) spaces where the spirit is nurtured, then (iii) there will be the freedom to soar to the heights of one's creative potential. In this chapter, we return to the coordinates to remind ourselves of some animating pathways, where "to *animate*" means, in this context, "to give life to or cause to come alive, to encourage or inspire, and to impart motion to" (our Collins English Dictionary definition,

DOI: 10.4324/9781003313601-8

1991, p. 60). Together with the teachers and kaiako, we were able to recognise creative storying and re-storying—linking to past knowledge and histories—for fostering *creative capacities* in contexts in which children, tamariki, were thinking with materials: as future poets, crafts-people, artists, teachers, kaiako, and kaumatua themselves. Reminding us of the discussions from Getzels and Csikszentmihalyi and Craft in earlier chapters, Richard Sennett was thinking about craftspeople working with materials when he said (Sennett, 2008, p. 9):

> Every good craftsman conducts a dialogue between concrete practices and thinking; this dialogue evolves into sustaining habits, and these habits establish a rhythm between problem solving and problem finding.

We also considered Dewey's *principle of continuity of experience* as a "criterion of discrimination" to describe one of the ways in which creative capacities might become an ongoing habit.

> The basic characteristic of habit is that every experience enacted and undergone modifies the one who acts and undergoes, while this modification affects, whether we wish it or not, the quality of subsequent experiences. …
>
> Collateral learning in the way of enduring attitudes, of likes and dislikes, may be and often is much more important than the spelling lesson or lesson in geography or history that is learned. For these attitudes are fundamentally what count in the future. The most important attitude that can be formed is that of desire to keep on learning.
>
> (Dewey 1938, pp. 26–27, 49)

Here, we define Dewey's "desire to keep on learning" as an aspect of *curiosity*. Creative capacities *carry on*, and we began to develop the theory that during visits to museums, while the tamariki (children) were *animating* the exhibits in personal and cultural ways, they were also becoming apprentice kaitiaki (trustees) not only for the taonga (treasured objects) in the museums, but also for *creative capacities*, the *animating*. In this chapter, we make a progressive argument for this, adapting Cultural Anchor 2, Cultural Anchor 3 and Cultural

Anchor 4. The fourth anchor arrives at kaitiakitanga and trusteeship, to suggest pathways for a creative capacity building when young children visit museums. Cultural Anchor 1 was the topic in Chapter 7.

Three pathways describe a developing creative capacity building over time

A first pathway for creative capacity building over time (see Figure 8.1) is adapted from Cultural Anchor 2:

> **whakamana/empowerment**, where tamariki and children are sharing the direction of the pathway. This follows *enduring attitudes* (Dewey, 1938, p. 49); specifically, in this case, guided by the tamariki (children) *being curious*.

A second pathway for creative capacity building over time (see Figure 8.2) is adapted from Cultural Anchor 3:

> **A reification** for stories of creative capacities in practice. This follows the supporting of *te reo, language competence* as a curriculum priority, and *portfolios that exemplify the hopes and aspirations of the people*

A third pathway for creative capacity building over time (see Figure 8.3) is adapted from Cultural Anchor Four:

Kaitiakitanga and trusteeship.

In this case, tamariki (children) become **kaitiaki (trustees) for animating**, finding their own creative spaces in the *coordinates of creative capacity building* whereby taonga are animated. The four coordinates chapters described this animating, whereby materials and taonga anchored the creativity and enabled some 'astonishing thinking' (Hutchins, 2005, p. 1562). And, like the stars of Matariki, which early Polynesian explorers used to *skilfully and wisely navigate pathways* in their double-hulled canoes 'across the greatest expanse of water on the planet'.

(Matamua, 2017, p. 2)

Pathway 1: Whakamana/empowerment

> *Whakamana (empowerment)* is a first way forward for creative capacity building: a pedagogy that is supported by curiosity and learning dispositions.

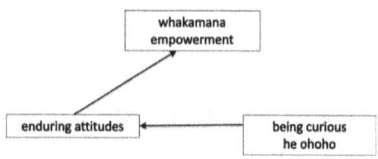

Figure 8.1 Whakamana/empowerment.

In Chapter 2, we introduced "whakamana/empowerment" to become part of the Cultural Anchor 2 triangle that included the development of being curious, *e ohooho*, (emphasised as a significant commitment for Wharekura, total immersion Māori Language secondary schools, established in the 1990s, in Te Aho Matua, a Ministry of Education (2008) guiding document) as an "enduring attitude" or disposition. Empowerment is the pedagogy, enabling an environmental encounter between kaiako (teachers), taonga (treasured objects) and tamariki (children) that exemplifies *curiosity*.

Whakamana/empowerment is one of the Aotearoa New Zealand early childhood curriculum principles in Te Whāriki, the national curriculum.

> Mā te whāriki e whakatō te kaha ki roto i te mokopuna, ki te ako, kia pakari ai ana tipu. (e whakatō te kaha: a cultivating of strength)
>
> Early childhood curriculum empowers the child to learn and grow.
> (Ministry of Education, 2017, p. 18)

That national early childhood curriculum, introduced in Chapter 1, includes the following comments in its explanation of "whakamana" (Ministry of Education, 2017, p. 18): "In an empowering curriculum, children have agency to create and act on their own ideas, develop knowledge and skills in areas that interest them and, increasingly, to make decisions and judgments on matters that relate to them".

Possibility thinking: Problem finding and problem honing

When the children visited museums, *curiosity* in practice included "possibility thinking", as a key feature of creative capacity building explored and highlighted by Anna Craft (2012, 2013). Anna Craft's writing about creativity was introduced in Chapter 1: she was also emphasising culture, and arguing for the value of a pedagogy that takes a "childhood as empowered" narrative (2013, p. 130) in a paper about digital technologies entitled "Childhood, possibility thinking and wise, humanising educational futures". She invites educators and policy-makers to "frame practice in relation to technology as *empowering* while recognising but not being driven by the risks" (p. 130). She describes "four P's" of digital childhood as plurality, participation, playfulness and possibility thinking, and she had argued much earlier that "at the heart of all creativity is possibility thinking—which drives creativity in different ways in different domains" (Craft, 2005, p. 36). She added in the 2013 paper that:

> Possibility thinking involves finding and honing problems.
>
> Wise humanising creativity is also informed by the notion of wise, creative trusteeship (Craft, 2008) positioned against marketized, individualized and culture blind creativity and embracing creative stewardship towards the collective good.
>
> (Craft, 2013, p. 128)

In Chapter 2, we described research on the value of teachers not always being certain, opening up opportunities for children to have the readiness and inclination—to be empowered—to express their own viewpoints and initiatives.

In Chapter 5, where the tamariki and kaiako were together *imagining possibilities,* problem finding and problem solving was introduced. Sometimes, the "finding" came first; sometimes the "solving"; in each case, original viewpoints and creative initiatives were enabled, and *whakamana*—and participation—is supported. Etienne Wenger, in his 1998 book on Communities of Practice, adds "participation" to "empowerment" commenting that "information, by itself, removed from forms of participation, is not knowledge" (p. 220). He adds

> What makes information knowledge—what makes it empowering— is the way in which it can be integrated within an identity of participation. When information does not build up to an identity of participation, it remains alien. Literal, fragmented, unnegotiable. It is not just that it is disconnected from other pieces of relevant information, but that it fails to translate into a way of being in the world coherent enough to be enacted in practice. Therefore, to know in practice is to have a certain identity so that information gains the coherence of a form of participation.
>
> (Wenger, 1998, p. 220)

Museum visits by the children at Mana Tamariki and Tai Tamariki combined information gathering with participation. In Chapter 3 (e rangahau ana—information gathering), Rakei te Kura was encouraged to ask for information from an artist who was constructing an exhibit at the local art gallery. Although he was initially shy to interact with the artist, he was encouraged to engage in a conversation, and the artist replied in detail about the cultural significance of the work. Following this, he drew his own parallel picture, including features of the work he had watched being developed several weeks earlier, while adding his own creative features. During a visit to a dinosaur exhibition with the Tai Tamariki Kindergarten, when Jeanette was a participant observer, Jack was gathering information about the meteor event that destroyed the dinosaurs and their families; a participating event was included and a conversation indicated how engaged he was because of that.

A museum visit in Chapter 4 (e whakawhanaunga ana/growing a relationship) enabled Taumaihiroa on every visit to the local museum, to search out, focus on, and draw her favourite taonga. She sat down with her drawing book and, during a number of visits over four to five months, she drew this taonga, an indigenous kite, drawing it differently each time. On the day she was recorded, she had included Tawhirimatea (the energy force, god of wind) and Tamanuiterā (the sun), as she apparently worked on solving the problem she had set herself: to express the spirit of, and to animate, the taonga.

In Chapter 5 (e waihanga ana—imagination), while creating their version of the Okatia pou (a ceremonial artwork that tells the story of Okatia, a spiritual being, carved for the museum in the 1980s), the tamariki were creatively problem finding *and* creatively problem solving. Rawhiti had set himself a problem of painting an outline of a gourd, then adding koru designs within the outline, and then filling in the lines with black colour. However, the process of this problem solving created a new problem: the paint pen draws a wider line than he plans and there is not enough room left for the koru (spiral pattern) design. He leaves frustrated that day but returns the next day with a solution to his problem.

At Tai Tamariki, two episodes in Chapter 5 (imagining—e waihanga ana) described Sarah thinking from the material, implicitly both finding and solving the problems she had while interacting with the dinosaur exhibit. Sarah was "standing her ground" and pursuing her own animating pathway, on two separate occasions, even when teachers questioned the sense of her mode of expressing, and interacting with, the dinosaur exhibit: she was perhaps becoming a kaitaki (trustee) for

Creative Capacity Building: A Going On 95

creative non-sense. She was also becoming ready for Trouble, and we are reminded of Bruner's persuasive notion that a good story will usually include Trouble; he commented that "It is the conversion of private Trouble into public plight that makes a well-wrought narrative so dangerous, so culturally essential" (Bruner, 2002, p. 35). There was a sense here of *whakamana* at work: the value for creative encounters of children being enabled to share the opportunities to be "in charge": as was Taumaihiroa, drawing and animating the indigenous kite via her actions.

Pathway 2: A reification of paki ako and learning stories that describe creative capacities in museums

A reification of paki ako and learning stories that describe creative capacities in museums, is a second way forward for creative capacity building. Stored in portfolios, these stories describe the creative capacity building, the journey, over time and learners as exemplifying the hopes and aspirations of the people; supported by te reo, language competence (widely defined) as a curriculum priority.

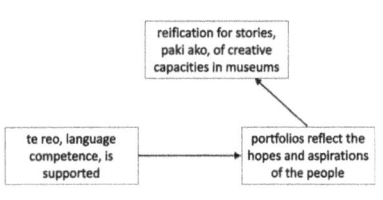

Figure 8.2 A reification of paki ako and learning stories.

In the early childhood centres, te reo Māori, and a wide range of languages were enhanced by a reification of stories: making them material. In the distant past, when te reo Māori was not a written language, creativity was also evident in the complex reification of stories—making them material, using a rich array of material arts. These arts continue to communicate *taonga Māori* in the hands of musicians, carvers, jewellery makers, painters, print-makers, potters, sculptors, and weavers, as well as writers and poets. In the early years' education context, in 1996 and the updated 2017 (see Chapter 1), the published curriculum set out in a document the aims, objectives and purposes of early childhood education. That New Zealand curriculum, *Te Whāriki* (introduced in Chapter 1), was based on the metaphor of a curriculum as a weaving, the principles and aims are notably illustrated as an "unfinished" whāriki "with loose strands still to be woven" (inside front cover). This notion that some of the detailed weaving of the aims and principles is uncertain, in the hands of whānau, kaiako and tamariki—families, teachers and children—as ongoing weavers, is a delightfully bold statement for a national curriculum document.

At Mana Tamariki, in Chapter 6 (e whakaahua ana—multiple modes), with in mind the freedom to soar to the heights of one's creative potential during a bush walk near the local mountains—in a place where the spirit would be nurtured, the kaiako recognised the purpose—to nurture the spirit—of the ritual, even when the "wrong" karakia (prayer chant) was recited by one of the children as tamariki and kaiako began a bush walk. She wrote in a warmly phrased paki ako (learning story) for his portfolio: "You showed your understanding that a ritual needed to be completed before entering the bush walk. You are a Māori child growing up speaking Māori and upholding Māori ways of being and doing".

Reifying and verifying the learning: Notebooks, project books, drawing books planning books, learning stories and paki ako

In this book, we have been especially interested in creative capacity *building*, in the documented examples of how creative outcomes were being realised, in diverse contexts and over time. These contexts included the multiple modes that enabled the re-telling of creative stories, thoughts and ideas in a range of material ways. In Chapter 2, the value of "semiotic materials" was described in Jay Lemke's (2000) discussion of "Across the Scales of Time: Artifacts, Activities, and Meanings in Ecosocial systems". He wrote (2000, p. 181) of the value of an object in a classroom:

> The notebook, as a material object with semiotic affordances, as a thing that can also be a sign, that *materially links two events across time and space* and so participates in a process on a much longer timescale than either the event of writing or the event of reading that particular note.

This material object uses writing and drawing as a way of anchoring the pedagogy and the learning. We noted that in both our education sites, ideas and understandings were documented in various material ways: the products of art by the tamariki (children), for instance, provided interpretations available to an audience. Other examples included, in Chapter 6, the children's drawings and paintings and Andrea's planning book. Taioperua's video production, also in Chapter 6, was an imaginatively reified request to the museum.

Learning stories and paki ako (Carr & Lee, 2012, 2019) that reify learning events as storying and re-storying were introduced in Chapter 1 of this book when Maiangi wrote up the theatre production for each of the child actors' portfolios; and Leanne wrote about Rakei te Kura's invention of a word, adding this story to all the portfolios in the kōhanga. The kaiako at Mana Tamariki explained that adding this example to all the children's portfolios (the tradition at Mana Tamariki) enacts the Aotearoa New Zealand early childhood curriculum principle of *whakamana*: "every child will experience an empowering curriculum that recognises and enhances their mana and supports them to enhance the mana of others". Paki ako and learning stories have a mixture of purposes and audiences; in Carr and Lee (2019), for example, the following purposes are discussed: being fair, recognising powerful frameworks, managing ambiguity, sharing responsibility with the learner, developing partnerships with whānau, and constructing progress. Examples in that 2019 book come from early years education programmes in eight different countries. And research findings in two mostly English-speaking kindergartens entitled "Teacher-talk about learning stories in New Zealand: a strategy for eliciting children's complex language" (Reese et al., 2019, pp. 12–13) concluded that:

> Learning stories have been found to be a valuable resource in supporting children to initiate interactions with teachers about events that are significant to them and their learning, where children have the opportunity to contribute to a shared memory recall as they tell their story.

At Mana Tamariki, the tamariki's role as kaitiaki includes to maintain the stories of his or her ancestors. In Chapter 6, a kaiako at Mana Tamariki writes a paki ako for all the children's portfolios about the children's walk in the Manawatu Gorge. Children can also dictate the stories about their own learning; in Chapter 6, one of the teachers at Tai Tamariki was sharing with four-year-old Rose the photographs she had taken during a museum visit to the dinosaur exhibition, and she invited Rose to dictate a Learning Story for her portfolio.

Learning stories and paki ako are housed in (variously named) Profile Books or Portfolios. Sometimes, as in Rose's example, these narrative assessments are dictated by the children. They provide the format for assessment of learning: set out in a narrative format rather than from a list of measured, levelled, narrow outcomes in early years centres in Aotearoa New Zealand. The curriculum states, writing about portfolios of children's learning, that: "Portfolios may include annotated photographs, children's art, recordings or transcripts of oral language, kaiako observations and learning stories" (Ministry of Education, 2017, p. 63). As Jerome Bruner (2002, p. 89) so cogently puts it:

> One truth is surely self-evident: for all that narrative is one of our evident delights, it is serious business. For better or worse, it is our preferred, perhaps even our obligatory medium for expressing human aspirations and their vicissitudes, our own, and those of others. Our stories also impose a structure, a compelling reality on what we experience, even a philosophical stance.

Narrative assessments as a sociocultural view of learning were developed in Aotearoa New Zealand. They are an assessment strategy that (i) acknowledges the distributed nature of learning, (ii) assessments as improvable objects and opportunities for developing a learning journey and (iii) assessments as boundary-crossing objects that mediate conversations across interested communities (Cowie & Carr, 2016).

Also reifying the museum-visit storying at Tai Tamariki were the children's Drawing Books, and one of the teachers, Andrea, documented her own teaching ideas and planning over time in a way that was available to the children: they were very interested in her Planning Book and added their own diagrams and drawings to it, thus creating a collaborative, conversational, reified, narrative that connected the creativity capacity building over time. Sarah, one of the keen four-year-old artists in that kindergarten, usually looked at earlier drawings in her Drawing Book before adding another. And for many children their Learning Storybooks—which contained photographs and were readily available for children and families to "read"—were also their Planning Books. Jay Lemke's (2000) discussion on "Across the Scales of Time: Artifacts, Activities, and Meanings in Ecosocial Systems" is relevant here. He argues that:

Creative Capacity Building: A Going On 99

(T)he properties of substance have meaning only in and through participation in processes, and those of artifacts through participation in networks of interdependent ecosocial processes, including human cultural practices.... My principle example is schooling in relation to identity development and cultural continuity.

(Lemke, 2000, p. 275)

Later, he adds:

The formation of identity, or even fundamental change in attitudes or habits of reasoning, cannot take place on short time scales. Even if short-term events contribute towards such changes, it is only the fact that they are *not* soon erased changes, do not quickly fade—that subsequent events do not reverse the change—that makes it count. It is the longer-term processes, including the effects of subsequent events, that determines for us the reality of basic human social development.

(Lemke, 2000, p. 282, italics in the original)

For Mana Tamariki and Tai Tamariki, the *reifying* of creative capacity-building events on short time scales ensures that they are not soon erased, and do not quickly fade

Pathway 3: Tamariki and children as kaitiaki for creative capacity building

A third way forward for creative capacity building. Children and tamariki as kaitiaki and trustees for **animating** the objects, enabled by the four *coordinates of creative capacity.*

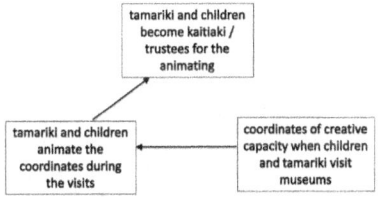

Figure 8.3 A third way forward for creative capacity building: Children and tamariki as Kaitiaki/Trustees for animating the objects in the museums.

In 2012, Tim Ingold proposed an ecology of materials that focuses on their enrolment in form-making processes, their histories (p. 427). He argued (p. 436) for a radical distinction between object and thing, referencing the philosopher Martin Heidegger (1971, pp. 165–182). The *object* is complete and ready-made: "We may interact with objects, but we cannot correspond with them.... Every *thing*, for Heidegger is a gathering of materials in movement.... and to witness a thing is to join with the processes of its ongoing formation" (Ingold, 2012, p. 436). In Aotearoa New Zealand, the equivalent for Māori is therefore *taonga*. Taonga are *animate*, although they are not necessarily material. Te reo, for instance, is a *taonga*, and museum visits by tamariki and kaiako who are only speaking te reo Māori to, and with, the taonga enable ongoing animating processes that sustain relationships.

In an imaginative way of describing an "enrolment in form-making processes" at the kindergarten before the dinosaur exhibition, in Chapter 6, Andrea (a teacher at Tai Tamariki) had developed a pedagogy of "Changing the Scale" that played with the notion that, as Gunther Kress had noted (2003, p. 107): "From the point of view of theory, one question is, what are the affordances of different modes, and how do different modes therefore realise meanings of a different kind?" Our participant observations suggested that these particular visits were more than information gathering, although this was certainly a feature. The responses noted and recorded a growing of relationships, an imagining of possibilities, and a multiplying of modes of expression.

Tamariki as kaitiaki for creative capacity building

A tentative vision of *kaitiakitanga* (trusteeship) in a wider context of a museum visit asks what might the young visitors hold in trust from a museum visit? This unravelling of different cultural storylines has created spaces for dialogue across differences. In each of the creative capacity coordinates chapters, we included examples and analysis of creative capacity building separately for the two culturally different sites: (i) Mana Tamariki kōhanga ki te kura—*ki tā te Māori titiro, ki tā te wairua Māori* (where there is a Māori perspective, there will be a Māori spirit or soul), and where a "going-on" includes a responsibility towards taonga on behalf of the iwi and ancestors that belong to them, and (ii) Tai Tamariki kindergarten (*pakeha* and *tauiwi*), where English is mostly spoken, and there are diverse cultural contexts and reference points. These education sites were described in Chapter 1.

The going-on in the dinosaur exhibition also includes a reverence and an awe enhanced by gathering knowledge about the dinosaurs, developing relationships, imagining them and their families, and reifying them in drawing; recognising them as amazing creatures that we will never meet but should remember, and a carry-on vision that includes other creatures who might be in peril with global warming and cataclysmic events. The Tai Tamariki children were also "adding on" to their gathering of information in animating ways: growing a relationship on their own terms, imagining possibilities, and making meaning by multiplying modes and representing perceptions. The Mana Tamariki tamariki, too, were adding to and handing on:

> The culture our ancestors brought with them was a taonga, treasure. It was a taonga they have handed on to us. It was a taonga that we in turn add to and hand on. Our culture, our taonga, does not end with us. It goes on, on into the future.
> (Adsett et al., 2005, p. 14)

We began to recognise a powerful sub-text that emerged from our examples: while the exhibition developers and the museum directors were acting as trustees for the taonga in their care, the tamariki and children (assisted by their kaiako and teachers) were going beyond information gathering to become trustees for *creative capacity building*. This included a creative *animating*: storying and restorying, often building on their prior knowledge in unusual ways. We return to John Dewey (1938), writing about "the principle of continuity":

> Every experience is a moving force. Its value can be judged only on the ground of what it moves forward and into. ... On one side, it is [the educator's] business to be alert to see what attitudes and habitual tendencies are being created. (pp. 31, 33)

Creative inter-animating

We extract some examples from the coordinates chapters, in response to what might have been Dewey's question for us; also in response to Linda Tuhiwai Smith's provocation, in Chapter 1: to "weave and unravel competing (cultural) storylines"; and to create "spaces for dialogue across difference"; and in response to our own question about tamariki (children) as kaitiaki (trustees) for creative capacity building.

We repeat a quote at the beginning of Chapter 1:

> Part of what makes cultural institutions like museums powerful forums for the creation of imagined communities is the fact

that they are potentially ideal public spaces where personal, private or autobiographical narratives come into contact with larger-scale, collective or national narratives in mutually inter-animating ways.

(Rowe et al., 2002, p. 98)

E rangahau ana—Gathering information

Learning/knowing part of the stories of the taonga/objects (Chapter 3). A recognition, from these particular visits, that there are interesting and vivid cultural and science stories attached to the taonga. The children's re-storying was enabled; their curiosity was enhanced and their problem finding via questioning and sympathetic enacting was recognised and enabled.

E whakawhanaunga ana—Growing relationships

Re-storying and restoring taonga/objects to life (Chapter 4). The sympathetic re-enacting continued, also reified in drawing, as in Chapter 3. Vivid storying and re-storying—from Mana Tamariki, accompanying several drawings over several visits—was enabled here too. One of the teachers at Tai Tamariki illustrated possibility thinking with materials—"changing the scale is quite useful"—and children were learning the value of, copying in their own way, the problem finding and problem solving.

E waihanga ana—Imagining possibilities

Imagination is wrapped around information about the taonga/objects (Chapter 5). The tamariki at Mana Tamariki were creating their own *pou,* an indigenous post/pole representing the story of Okatia creating the Manawatu Gorge. As a collective they were imagining, and incorporating in practice, what Okatia would possibly need on the journey. At Tai Tamariki, Sarah was illustrating the value of creating a "person-plus" (Perkins, 1993, 2009) when confronting a (scary) dinosaur, in this case the "plus" was her drawing book and a bag of fabrics, in order to, in effect, create a measure of empowerment.

E whakaahua ana—Multiplying modes

Re-presenting perceptions and encouraging further stories (Chapter 6). Expressing their ideas in multiple modes, tamariki were making meaning in mode-specific ways. We were reminded of the Reggio

Emilia schools, and the multiple communication modes illustrated in Chapter 6: drawing, painting, collage and film-making (during and after the construction of the pou), the beginning of a journey with a karakia, accessing information from books, constructing from "found objects" (an egg carton), and contributing to a recorded interview for a learning story.

Making sense by focusing on the small to make sense of the big

In both sites, the children were learning a number of ways to "be a museum visitor". From our examples, one of these was to focus on the small in order to make sense of the big: Sarah's drawings and fabric disguise, and Taumaihiroa's kite drawings illustrated this. Perhaps Taioperua, masterminding the construction of a video of the tamariki pou construction was illustrating this too: dividing the work for a big construction task, creatively recognising its smaller pieces, and knowing the children well enough to assign the tasks.

In Chapter 2, we suggested a metaphor for the *coordinates* in this book: a "star cluster" as a guide for the space where the spirit is nurtured and creativity will be inspired. In the southern hemisphere, the Matariki cluster of stars provided guiding coordinates for early travellers across the Pacific Ocean, although they don't bump into each other and connect together, as do our coordinates. Edwin Hutchins argued for material anchoring's stabilizing role, to assist with "astonishing thinking". We have seen in Chapters 3–6 that our coordinates, anchoring the children's interactions with exhibits, had a special role in creative capacity building: to *animate* the museum exhibits in various ways: by gathering information about them, growing relationships with them, imagining possibilities, and multiplying the modes with which to describe and ascribe them. During museum visits, children (tamariki) and teachers (kaiako) engage with exhibits by constructing these *animating* encounters that connect the little and the big narratives. This became a theme for this book, and our discussions also resonate with the work of Shawn Rowe et al. (2002). Writing about "Linking Little Narratives to Big Ones: Narrative and Public Memory in History Museums", they describe (p. 109) the ways in which official museum narratives come into contact with cultural narratives produced by visitors. They note two ways in which this happens:

1   In the first, elements of the official narrative representations serve as jumping-off points for what might be called private memory practices or performances of self.

2   In the second, visitors also draw on their personal experiences … to illustrate or support or potentially deny the truth or authority of the official account.

This is, for us, a discussion about the difference between a gathering of information and the creative capacity building in Chapters 4–6. However, even in Chapter 3, a gathering of information was animated when Jack was acting out the demise of the dinosaurs by the meteor, apparently an act of sympathy and caring. Rowe et al. (2002) also add (p. 109), "We view our discussion as only an initial step in a broader discussion of how little narratives can come into contact with big ones". And they conclude that "The story is likely to get much more complicated than anything we have envisioned here". In our discussions, in this book, perhaps we have contributed to those ongoing complications.

A going-on of the children's capacity building coordinates

We have continued to think in triangles, the title of Chapter 2 and the framing for Chapter 7. During our discussions about connecting the four coordinates together and imagining how they might carry the creative capacity building on, Leanne, one of the authors of this book and a kaiako at Mana Tamariki kōhanga ki te kura, devised the idea of folding up the four coordinates, together, as *tapatoru* (triangles) into a wider folded *matawhārite*, that is, a three-dimensional shape, a tetrahedron. She describes the complicated picture of ongoing creative capacity building as the four interacting coordinates "tumbling down a slope". Since the complexity of a three-dimensional folded triangle cannot be included in this two-dimensional (written) account, she commented:

> I thought about what coordinate will go in which triangle remembering that no one coordinate is more important than the other, and chose gathering information and growing relationships to be in the bottom triangles as a foundation. As we use the word *building*, I use the word *foundation* as the base and reading through the transcripts I found it was mostly *information gathering* and the *growing relationships* that are the foundation. Through *multiplying modes* and moving across the *information gathering* and *relationships growing*, the *imagining possibilities* begins and develops. I also like the imagining possibilities at the top, ready to fly away.
>
> (Leanne Apera-Ngaha)

Creative Capacity Building: A Going On   105

This tumbling tetrahedron, or "folded" triangle, made up of small triangles illustrates the creative capacity-building pedagogy, the animating via the interactions in the coordinates, and the ecosocial framing. When children visit museums over time with guidance and agency, they form relationships with taonga and artefacts which open up spaces for possibilities and revisions of their ways of being and belonging and creative capacity building. Here is Leanne's suggestion:

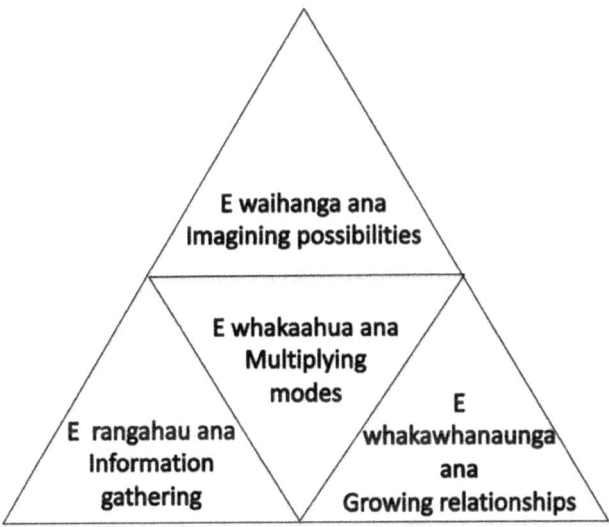

Figure 8.4 Tumbling tetrahedron, or "folded" triangle.

This tetrahedron, or "folded" triangle made up of small triangles, emphasises the creative capacity-building pedagogy and the ecosocial framing. It reminds us of one of the teacher's policies, described in Chapter 4: "When I get stuck for ideas, changing the scale's quite useful. When you've got big things, making them small ...... when you've got small things making it big". And in a book entitled "*Māori and the Environment: Kaitiaki*", based on an address to the World Heritage Committee's Pacific Workshop, held in Turangi, Aotearoa New Zealand in 2007, Mason Durie describes a dynamic spiral from the small to the large at the heart of indigeneity (Figure 8.4).

> Underlying the world views of indigenous peoples and at the heart of indigeneity, it is possible to identify an 'ecological spiral'. The spiral is basically about relationships and especially relationships

that are complementary and mutually reinforcing. The spiral moves from the small to the large..... Stone, for instance, whether in a natural state or used for construction cannot be fully understood without recognising the wider environment within which it lies.

(Durie, 2010, p. 242, 243)

References

Adsett, S., Whiting, C., Karetu, T., Lardelli, D., & Ihimaera, W. (2005). Mataora the living space. In S. Adsett & C. Whiting (Eds.), *Mataroa the living face: Contemporary Maori art, te waka toi*. Bateman.

Bruner, J. (2002). *Making stories: Law, literature, life*. Harvard University Press.

Carr, M., & Lee, W. (2012). *Learning stories: Constructing learner identities in early education*. Sage.

Carr, M., & Lee, W. (2019). *Learning stories in practice*. Sage.

Cowie, B., & Carr, M. (2016). Narrative assessment: A sociocultural view. In M. A. Peters (Ed.), *Encyclopedia of educational philosophy and theory*. 10.1007/978-981-287-532-7396-1

Craft, A. (2005). *Creativity in schools: Tensions and dilemmas*. Routledge.

Craft, A. (2008). Tensions in creativity and education: Enter wisdom and trusteeship? In A. Craft., H. Gardner, & G. Claxton (Eds.), *Creativity, wisdom, and trusteeship: Exploring the role of education* (pp.16–34). Corwin.

Craft, A. (2013). Childhood, possibility thinking and wise, humanising educational futures. *International Journal of Educational Research, 61*, 126–134. 10.1016/j.ijer.2013.02.005

Dewey, J. (1938/1959). *Experience and education*. MacMillan.

Durie, M. (2010). Outstanding universal value: How relevant is indigeneity? In R. Selby, P. Moore, & M. Mulholland (Eds.), *Māori and the environment: Kaitiaki* (pp. 239–251). Huia.

Heidegger, M. (1971). *Poetry, language, thought* (Transl. A. Hofstadter). Harper & Rowe.

Hutchins, E. (2005). Material anchors for conceptual blends. *Journal of Pragmatics, 37*, 1555–1577. http://www.cogsci.ucsd.edu/~faucon/BEIJING/hutchins.pdf

Ingold, T. (2011). *Being alive: Essays on movement, knowledge and description*. Routledge.

Ingold, T. (2012). Toward an ecology of materials. *Annual Review of Anthropology, 41*, 427–442. 10.1146/annurev-anthro-081309-145920

Kress, G. (2003). *Literacy in the new media age*. Routledge.

Lemke, J. (2000). Across the scales of time: Artifacts, Activities, and meanings in ecosocial sytems. *Mind, Culture, and Activity, 7*(4), 273–290. 10.1207/S15327884MCA0704_03

Matamua, R. (2017). *Matariki: The star of the year*. Huia.

Ministry of Education. (2008). *Te Aho Matua o ngā kura kaupapa Māori and an explanation in English.*

Ministry of Education. (2017). *Te Whariki: Early childhood curriculum.* Education Counts. https://www.education.govt.nz/assets/Documents/Early-Childhood/Te-Whariki-Early-Childhood-Curriculum-ENG-Web.pdf

Perkins, D. N. (1993). Person-plus: A distributed view of thinking and learning. In G. Salaomon (Ed.), *Distributed cognitions: Psychological and educational considerations* (pp. 88–110). England: Cambridge University Press.

Perkins, D. N. (2009). *Making learning whole.* Jossey-Bass.

Reese, E., Gunn, A., Bateman, A., & Carr, M. (2019). Teacher-talk about learning stories in New Zealand: A strategy for eliciting children's complex language. *Early Years.* 10.1080/09575146.2019.1621804

Rowe, S. M., Wertsch, J. W., & Kosyaeva, T. Y. (2002). Linking little narratives to big ones: Narrative and public memory in history museums. *Culture & Psychology, 8*, 96.

Sennett, R. (2008). *The craftsman.* Penguin.

Wenger, E. (1998). *Communities of Practice: Learning, meaning and identity.* Cambridge University Press.

Index

Adsett, S. 80
anchors: cultural 20–21, 40, 54, 91; material 20, 50, 54, 66, 78, 97
animating 9, 21, 89, 90, 101–103

bicultural 2, 6
Bruner, J. 11–12, 15, 20, 23, 28–29, 95, 98

carry on 90
Claxton, G. 23, 27–28, 80, 85
Craft, A. 6, 12, 27–28, 84–85, 92, 93
creativity 71
creativity capacity building 10, 30, 39, 40, 43, 84, 85, 87, 90–91, 96; definition 13, 57; encounters 30, 50, 86
coordinates 30, 33
context 3, 96
cultural anchors
curriculum: early childhood 7, 10, 26, 28, 45–46, 92, 96; school 92

Dewey, J. 9, 90, 101
dispositions 10, 23, 57, 85, 92
Durie, M. 1, 9, 46–47, 89, 105–106

ecosocial framing 8, 9, 105
Eisner, E. 78–79
Empowerment/whakamana 22, 92

forum 57

Gardner, H. 27–28
genealogy 50
"going on" 27, 30, 78, 104

Hutchins, E. 20, 53

imagination 12, 13, 56, 59, 66, 102
Ingold, T. 9–10, 21, 46, 54, 69, 89, 100

Kress, G. 72, 86, 100

learning stories/paki ako 24–25, 95–98
Lemke, J. 9, 27, 96, 98–99

mode/multi-modal 71
Mikaere, A. 45, 50

narratives 71, 98; assessment 98

paki ako/learning stories 24–25, 95–98
Perkins, D 23, 85
possibility thinking 92

Reece E. 97
Reggio Emilia 71
reifying 96–99
Rinaldi, C. 71

Sennett, R. 90
surprise 58

tetrahedron 105; tumbling 105
treasures/ taonga 3, 10, 21, 33, 46, 95, 99–102
trusteeship (kaitiakitanga) 27–28, 39, 40, 43, 62, 66, 81, 87, 88, 91, 99–101

Wenger, E. 93
whakamana/empowerment 7, 13, 22, 24, 37, 39, 86, 91
wisdom 22, 27–28, 85

For Product Safety Concerns and Information please contact our EU representative GPSR@taylorandfrancis.com
Taylor & Francis Verlag GmbH, Kaufingerstraße 24, 80331 München, Germany

www.ingramcontent.com/pod-product-compliance
Lightning Source LLC
Chambersburg PA
CBHW051755230426
43670CB00012B/2305